The repair of historic timber structures

The repair of historic timber structures

David Yeomans

T Thomas Telford

Published by Thomas Telford Publishing, Thomas Telford Ltd, 1 Heron Quay, London E14 4JD.

Distributors for Thomas Telford books are
USA: ASCE Press, 1801 Alexander Bell Drive, Reston, VA 20191-4400, USA
Japan: Maruzen Co. Ltd, Book Department. 3–10 Nihonbashi 2-chome, Chuo-ku, Tokyo 103
Australia: DA Books and Journals, 648 Whitehorse Road, Mitcham 3132, Victoria

First published 2003

A catalogue record for this book is available from the British Library

ISBN: 0 7277 3213 7

Typeset by Ian Kingston Editorial Services, Nottingham, UK
Printed in Great Britain by MPG Books, Bodmin

Contents

Contents

Preface

England has a surprising number of timber-framed buildings, many hidden behind brick facings and often considerably altered over the years (Figure 1). Because they mostly date from before 1700 they are normally listed buildings, and listed building consent must be obtained for their alteration. At the same time, many are in urban areas so that their continuing economic life often requires that they be adapted and upgraded to suit modern requirements if they are to accommodate present-day functions, whether as houses, offices, shops or restaurants.

Figure 1

A larger proportion of our building stock comprises 18th and 19th century buildings, and although these are seen as masonry buildings their structures still depend to a large extent on their timber floors and internal walls. They too often require upgrading to suit modern requirements, involving alterations or simply an increase in floor loading. These two kinds of historic building involve quite different traditions of carpentry, using different materials (the first native oak; the second imported softwood), and this book will deal with the analysis and repair of the timber building structures from both these traditions.

The intention of the book is to act as a guide for those involved in the structural assessment and repair of timber in buildings. While it discusses the quantitative analysis of structures that will be of concern to engineers, it also provides qualitative descriptions of structural behaviour for architects and carpenters concerned with these buildings, and discusses details of repairs. The approach has been to look at forces within typical structures so that in examining an actual structure the conservator will have an idea of where stresses are likely to be high and so which areas should be most carefully examined. Therefore the sequence adopted in the text has been that which would be used in calculations, starting with the roof and working downward through the structure. In a number of cases alternative load paths are considered, and the level of confidence that may be placed in the results of the calculations is discussed. To do this we will consider several typical structures. In each case the original structural layout will be examined, although the conservator today will often be dealing with buildings that have been altered and for which both the structures and the loading will have been changed.

These structures often present difficulties in analysis and may not conform to modern code requirements. Not only are they sometimes rather complex, they also present many unknown factors: the relative stiffness of members, for example. As well as the difficulty that the structural behaviour of original carpentry techniques has not received much investigation and is certainly not covered by modern codes, neither are some of the repair methods in use anticipated by these codes. It will therefore be necessary to discuss some of these repair methods and the standards that might be applied. These are structures which, even without deliberate alteration, may have changed over time, so that the present load paths may not be those that were active when the buildings were first built. This means that we may have to consider alternative load paths in the analysis of the structure. It may even be that, in carrying out the repairs, load paths may be changed yet again. Indeed, the choice for the conservator when faced with a changed structure may be whether to stabilize it in its changed state, to restore it to its original state or to introduce still further changes. These are issues that have been discussed elsewhere (Yeomans and Smith, 2000) and come under what might be called the philosophy of conservation. This is not something that will be discussed in detail here, and the text will be confined to technical matters. However, it is important to emphasise that a clear conservation policy needs to be established at the beginning of any project, bearing in mind the technical limitations.

While the book includes the quantitative analysis of structures that will be of concern to engineers, the intention is to provide sufficient qualitative descriptions of structural behaviour for readers with limited structural knowledge to be able to follow the issues being discussed. To cater for this broad readership, including architects, structural engineers and carpenters, some of the more detailed and quantitative material has been separated from the main text, and the following methods have been adopted:

- The behaviour of each structure is first described qualitatively before any numerical considerations.
- Wherever possible the behaviour of structures has been simplified so that they may be treated as statically determinate.

While this does involve some approximations, the effect of this on the results is discussed. It is also worth noting that the author's view is that these structures do not lend themselves easily to modern methods of analysis and the application of computer techniques. The properties of the sections used in early timber-framed buildings can seldom be specified with great accuracy, and they may change considerably in the length of the member. While that is not true to the same degree with later softwood structures, the behaviour of joints and the accuracy of carpentry are always problematic. Often an indeterminate analysis will give a subtler and possibly accurate picture, but it is necessary to explore the effect of varying timber properties and connection characteristics. In one or two instances the use of computer analysis has been suggested as a means of exploring the possible behaviour of the structure rather than to obtain definitive results. In all such cases the engineer should be careful to ensure that the model used bears some resemblance to the behaviour and condition of the actual structure.

Some elementary understanding of structural behaviour has been assumed in presenting the calculations. This is:

- An understanding of the resolution of forces.
- A knowledge of moments of forces, especially where used in determining reactions on simple structures.
- A simple understanding of bending moments and the calculation of moments on a simply supported beam.
- A knowledge of the relationship between bending moments and stresses in a rectangular section.

In a number of cases text will be found in boxes to distinguish it from the main body of the text. This will be a piece of structural theory or a calculation that is not essential for a qualitative understanding of the structure. The intention is that readers who may not be comfortable with structural analysis may omit these parts of the text without undue loss and perhaps return to them later.

However, before tackling the structural analysis we need to consider some fundamental issues: the nature of the materials used in these early structures and how they differ from modern materials, the method of assessing individual timbers and the nature of the joints between them. In some cases it will be useful to refer to research work that has been carried out on aspects of these structures which may be relevant to their analysis but which could not be included in the interest of brevity. There is a brief chapter on the process of surveying historic structures that could be the subject of a book in itself. But the need for a thorough and timely structural survey can hardly be over-emphasised, particularly because structures of this period have so often been altered and the engineer will seldom be dealing with the pure forms described here.

In dealing with two distinct carpentry traditions, early oak frames and later softwood structures, the analysis of structures falls into two main parts. In each part actual structures will be described and calculations carried out to show the kind of stress levels which may be expected and, where appropriate, repair methods will also be discussed. Surviving early oak framed structures are largely domestic and agricultural buildings, while softwood was increasingly used for industrial and commercial buildings during the late 18th and 19th centuries, with consequent increases in the spans required. Of course there are church buildings of both periods.

Chapter 1 deals briefly with the harvesting, conversion and supply of timbers as well as discussing the properties of the principal species used. This considers moisture movement, resistance to decay and strength properties of both native oak used in early timber frames and the imported softwoods of more recent structures. Construction of the basic timber frames of both periods is then described in Chapter 2. It is then appropriate to discuss the behaviour of joints (Chapter 3), because these are perhaps the most important influence on the behaviour of the original structures as well as being important in repairs. In Chapter 4 the load transmission in various structures is described qualitatively. Some simple calculations are introduced at this stage to give an idea of the nature and magnitude of the forces. Chapters 5 and 6 consider the detailed calculation of the behaviour of some basic structures and the text is supported by a number of spreadsheets. Chapters 7 and 8 of the book discuss the design of repairs and the survey of structures.

Both imperial and metric measures have been used in the text. The former are commonly used by carpenters, partly because these were the units in which the structures that we are discussing were made and partly because it is simply easier to measure in these units when surveying an existing building built before 1969. However, metric units are used as well because these are the units used for present day codes of practice, and therefore all loads and stresses are expressed in metric units. In presenting the calculations a distinction has been made between measured or assumed values and those which have been calculated as a result of those values. The former are indicated with the symbol '@', while the latter have the normal '=' before them.

In the calculations and examples CP3 Chapter V is referred to although BS 6399 has been available for some time. CP3 Chapter V has not been withdrawn and the reason for its use here is that it provides a very much simpler method for determining wind loads, a method that could possibly be used by architects or carpenters to obtain preliminary figures. Note, however, that the two codes use different basic wind speeds as the starting point for calculations. CP3 Chapter V uses the 3 second gust speed, which is higher than the hourly mean used by BS 6399.

Acknowledgements

My thanks to my colleague Andrew Smith for his valuable help and suggestions, to Peter McCurdy and his staff for all that I have learnt from them, to Carl Ozelton for helping with the code of practice, and to Lawrance Hurst and Andor Gomme for supplying information on specific buildings.

1

The materials

Oak was the preferred and most commonly used structural timber until the 17th century, although some inferior materials, often elm, are sometimes found in these early buildings. Therefore oak is the material assumed here for timber-framed buildings. Following the Fire of London, imported softwood was increasingly used for building. Timber imported from the Baltic countries was principally pine (*Pinus sylvestris*) and spruce (*Picea abies*), although at the time both were called fir. Of course the change to softwood did not occur everywhere at the same time. Oak continued to be used in some parts of the country because in some districts, especially away from good water transport, oak might have been more readily available than imported softwood and so might have persisted longer in general use. Also oak continued to be preferred for its durability, and so was used for better work and for some particular components. For example, oak roofing laths were preferred to fir because they were more durable. Oak was also recommended for the king posts of roof trusses even though fir might be used for the other members. This was possibly because a stronger timber was thought preferable for this important member of the roof.

Oak harvesting, seasoning and conversion

Oak woodlands were managed to produce a supply of timber. Coppices were formed by leaving the stumps of felled trees to sprout and produce the 'underwood', i.e. the wood under the standing trees, and this was regularly cropped. Coppiced wood produced fairly straight, knot-free timbers, although of limited size and with a fairly large proportion of the less durable sapwood. This was trimmed to a square section by axe and then halved by sawing down its length. The halved and fairly small scantling timbers that were obtained in this way were used for small wall studs, rafters and floor joists. There would often be some wane on these timbers, but more seriously today we find a loss of sapwood at the arrises because of beetle attack. The pith is also susceptible to fungal decay and one often finds loss of this in the upper surface of rafters.

Large section timbers were obtained by selecting a tree of an appropriate size and using the trunk and branches, which if left square as trimmed with the axe are known as boxed heart. These too might be halved for some structural members, such as roof purlins and braces. Tree trunks naturally contain knots, and it might not always have been possible for the carpenter to obtain knot-free timber, so that its quality was variable. In later buildings it might also have been difficult to obtain the best quality timber and, apart from the use of inferior species, sawn timbers of poor quality are sometimes seen with excessive slope of grain.

Softwood supplies

As an imported timber, softwood could either be brought into the country in logs or could be sawn in the country of origin; both were done. It is apparent from contemporary accounts and from inspection of some 18th century structures that logs were imported for sawing in Britain, although timber sawn in the country of origin before drying should have less checking (see below) than timber dried in the log and sawn here. There is every reason to expect imported timbers to have been brought in ready-sawn. Norway certainly had power sawmills, while sawing in England had to be by hand because of the suppression of power sawmills (Cooney, 1991). Also, in the early 19th century importing of unsawn material would have been discouraged because of a differential import duty in favour of sawn timber (Yeomans, 1989).

Imported softwood was generally named after the port of origin rather than by species; thus one finds references to Memel, Riga and Christiania (Oslo) fir. The different naming is significant because the properties of *Pinus sylvestris*, which was the principal species, vary noticeably with the conditions of growth, and the hinterland supplying these ports was different. These were the early sources of supply, but during the 18th century timber also became available from Britain's North American colonies and, in spite of some prejudice against it, this source was encouraged by differential import duties towards the end of the 18th century. The effect of North American supplies was naturally to introduce different species, although contemporary names are confusing and it is often difficult to tell from building accounts or other documents which species were referred to. It is likely that the relative ease with which these new sources penetrated the market in Britain would have depended upon the nearness to particular ports: north American timbers are more likely to have found favour close to Liverpool, while the use of Baltic timbers persisted longer close to London.

Other materials

Iron strapping was used extensively in combination with softwood for roof trusses from the mid-17th century onwards, and during the 19th century iron castings and wrought iron tie bars came into common use. This represented a shift from simple blacksmith's work to better engineered products. With this change also went a change in some of the metal fasteners used. It is not possible to discuss the properties of these because no work has been done to assess the quality and hence the strength characteristics of the materials used. However, no failures in these components have been observed.

Another change that occurred in the 19th century was the use of tropical hardwoods obtained from the colonies. These were not often used but do occasionally appear in special circumstances – in long-spanning roof trusses for example. Tropical hardwoods were used for components of long-spanning roof trusses built by Robert Smirke in 1813 for the Custom House, London which have a clear span of 62' 7" (19 m). A detail of this is shown in Figure 3.18. When Smirke designed a new roof for the choir of York Minster after the original had been destroyed in a fire, he specified that teak should be used for the trusses. This was possibly for durability rather than for its strength, because the truss shown in his drawing[*] appears to be adequate for the span even had it been of softwood. However, the design also used iron plates to reinforce the supporting bearers at the wall plate.

Effect of shrinkage of timbers

As it dries, all timber shrinks across the grain, with negligible movement along the grain. This has an effect on both the individual members and on the behaviour of the building. The first observed effect is

---

[*] RIBA Drawings collection DC: J9/16.

that the outside of the timber, i.e. that exposed to the air, dries first and tries to shrink, while the inside of the timber remains wetter and so shrinks more slowly. The outside layers, prevented from shrinking by the wetter core, develop tensile forces, resulting in the shakes and drying checks that one sees in large timbers. Secondly, the shrinkage is different in each direction, with that tangential to the growth rings larger than the radial shrinkage. This difference exacerbates the splitting problem and causes cupping of boards.

Deterioration

A detailed account of the deterioration of timber has been given by Ridout (1999), so that this subject only needs to be discussed briefly here. As a naturally durable timber, the heartwood of oak resists both fungal and beetle attack. The nature of medieval timber frame construction also ensured that timbers were kept reasonably dry. However, the outer sapwood is vulnerable and the most common form of deterioration is from attack of the sapwood by furniture beetle, while the heartwood remains untouched. Once the frass has been removed, the timber underneath is likely to be sound so that, if necessary, one can simply calculate for a reduced section. Deathwatch beetle may attack the heartwood of oak, and the difficulty with this form of attack is that it is less visible at the surface. The other problem with deathwatch beetle is that the tunnels made by the beetle may affect the timber into which the fasteners for repairs are to be placed.

Some timbers might be subject to long-term wetting, and so be likely to decay. Obvious places for this are where there were adjacent buildings because, without the kind of flashing materials and details that were later used, water might penetrate between the two and be trapped. Exposed timber, although not continuously wet, may deteriorate because of frequent wetting over a long period, particularly in places where the end grain becomes wet. These include the ends of jettied joists and the feet of rafters. Also vulnerable are the joints, where water getting in will be taken up by the end grain of the timbers. Because there is no air circulation round the timber to carry away moisture vapour, once wet, timber in joints will tend to stay wet and so decay may well start in these areas.

Used in less exposed circumstances and protected from penetrating or rising damp in the masonry, softwood will remain in perfectly good condition. The vulnerable timbers are those in direct contact with masonry. These are the ends of beams built into walls, the bond timbers that were commonly built into brickwork, and wall plates and the ends of roof timbers where box gutters were used. None of the softwoods used would today be rated as durable timbers, but the more resinous woods were selected for conditions where there might be water penetration.

Strength properties

The strength of a piece of timber depends upon both its species and its grade, and for the convenience of present day engineering design timbers have been grouped according to these two factors into strength classes (see Appendix 1). This avoids the designer needing to have a detailed knowledge of the properties of individual species. However, the properties of the individual species and grades are still provided in the current design code and so can be used if required. The concern of the engineer will be to specify the strength class appropriate to the structural properties required: either the working stresses or the stiffness. Tables 1.1 and 1.2 give figures for the working stresses and stiffnesses of softwoods and hardwoods, respectively, extracted from Table 7 of BS 5268. There are higher grades, but these are unlikely to be of interest to most conservators unless repairing 19th century structures that used much higher grades of softwood or, unusually, imported hardwoods – possibly colonial hardwoods. Note that the higher grades of softwood are actually better than the lowest grade of hardwoods.

Oak is classed as a temperate hardwood, for which there are different grades, and the grading method used for oak is also different from that used for other timbers (see below). The properties of these are shown in Table 1.3. The THA and THB grades only apply to timbers with a cross-sectional area larger than 20 000 mm^2, corresponding to the main members in an oak-framed structure.

Because of the structure of wood, the basic stresses that any timber will carry depend upon the direction of load and upon the species. However, the growth characteristics of a particular timber, the presence of knots, slope of grain and drying checks may all reduce the load that can be carried. Strength grading is the process of estimating the overall effect of these characteristics within each piece of timber, and there are several reasons why it is important for conservators to have some knowledge and understanding of the grading process. While the conservator may specify a grade of timber required for repair or restoration

Strength class	Bending stress	Compression parallel to the grain	Compression perpendicular to the grain	Shear parallel to the grain	Mean modulus of elasticity	Minimum modulus of elasticity
C14	4.1	5.2	2.1	0.6	6800	4600
C16	5.3	6.8	2.2	0.67	8800	5800
C18	5.8	7.1	2.2	0.67	9100	6000
C22	6.8	7.5	2.3	0.71	9700	6500
C24	7.5	7.9	2.4	0.71	10800	7200
C27	10.0	8.2	2.5	1.1	12300	8200

Table 1.1 Properties of softwoods.

Strength class	Bending stress	Compression parallel to the grain	Compression perpendicular to the grain	Shear parallel to the grain	Mean modulus of elasticity	Minimum modulus of elasticity
D30	9.0	8.1	2.8	1.4	9500	6000
D35	11.0	8.6	3.4	1.7	10000	6500
D40	12.5	12.6	3.9	2.0	10800	7500

Table 1.2 Properties of hardwoods.

Strength class	Bending stress	Compression parallel to the grain	Compression perpendicular to the grain	Shear parallel to the grain	Mean modulus of elasticity	Minimum modulus of elasticity
TH1	9.6	9.3	4.0	2.0	12500	8500
TH2	7.8	8.4	4.0	2.0	10500	7000
THA	12.6	10.5	4.0	2.0	13500	10500
THB	9.1	9.0	4.0	2.0	12000	7500

Table 1.3 Properties of oak.

the resawing of a piece can alter its grade, and one should be clear why this is so. The conservator may need timbers that are in the standing building to be graded to allow their likely strength to be assessed so that the methods of grading become important. In some cases it may also be necessary to justify higher stresses than the grade of timber might suggest are possible, so that one needs to assess its strength where the stresses are highest. These issues will be dealt with as appropriate, but a general knowledge of grades is also useful.

The original British grading rules for structural timbers, first published in 1952 (CP112), were based on the size and position of knots visible on the surface of the timber. The strength properties for each species were obtained from tests on small clear specimens (see BS 373: 1929).[†] The result of tests on a large number of specimens is a histogram or distribution curve of results. As the results are 'normally' distributed it is possible to perform some simple statistical calculations on the values (Figure 1.1). A 'basic stress' was calculated from the distribution of the test results by taking the lower 1% value (that is, 99% of timber of that species would be stronger than the figure obtained) and then applying a safety factor of 2.25 for bending, tension and shear stresses. (A safety factor of 1.4 was used for compression stresses.) The grade stresses to be used in design were then calculated as percentages of the basic stress, the grade being dependent upon the size and position of

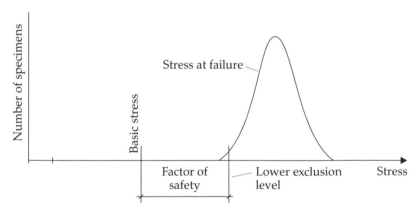

Figure 1.1 The statistical basis of working stresses. Originally based on small clear specimens, the 1% exclusion limit of the test results was taken and divided by the safety factor to obtain the basic stress given in CP112. Grade stresses were then a percentage of that.

---

† Work on the strengths of timber was first wanted for the design of aircraft frames and was not applied to building until much later.

the knots (see Appendix 2). The same method was used for all species and it is thus possible to derive a basic stress and grade stresses for any species not contained within the code's list of species from data on small clear specimens, providing test data is available; from Lavers (1969) for example.

Today oak is still graded in a similar way, although the number of grades has been reduced to four. Two of these are only applicable to the larger sections. Smaller timbers have two grades (TH1 and TH2) and for larger timbers there are also THA and THB grades. In Table 1.4 the allowable stresses for these are compared with the earlier CP112 working stresses, from which it is clear that for nearly equivalent strengths the modulus of elasticity has been increased.

While new timbers are graded by the supplier, this method can also be used on timbers in place within the building. Of course the grade of any piece of timber identifies the strength of the weakest part of that piece. One of the advantages of conservation work is that one is using small quantities of timber for known locations in the building. Thus, even if a given piece is not supplied as THA grade it may be possible to use it in such a way that it conforms to the requirements of THA grade where the stresses are highest.

Methods of grading softwoods have changed, as have the methods of specifying timbers. The 'knot area ratio' (KAR) method of grading was introduced with the publication of BS 4978 in 1973 that reduced the visual grades available to two: GS and SS. To avoid the need for engineers to specify both the species as well as the grade, combinations of species and grade were also grouped into strength classes. The Standard also changed the method by which the working stresses were determined (although this change has been largely invisible to most engineers, whose principal concern is just to have stresses that can be used in design). Permissible stresses are now determined by tests on graded timbers of commercially used sizes, with the allowable stresses in BS 5268 now obtained by taking the 5% value from the distribution curve, with a safety factor of 2.5 for bending stresses. This change has simplified the specification of materials for new building projects, but has not helped the conservator. The KAR method of grading depends upon knowing the position of the pith in any piece of timber, possible when grading new timbers but nearly always impossible when looking at timbers that have been built into a structure, so that conservators may still have to rely upon the old grading rules.

This means that while the grading of existing hardwood timber in the structure can be carried out using the rules set out in BS 5756 for grading hardwoods, the position with softwoods is less clear. The

9

Grade	Bending (N/mm²)	Tension, parallel (N/mm²)	Compression, parallel (N/mm²)	Compression, perpendicular (N/mm²)	Shear, parallel (N/mm²)	E, mean (N/mm²)	E, minimum (N/mm²)
Basic	20.7	20.7	15.2	4.48	3.1		
75	13.8	13.8	10.3	3.79	2.07	9700	5200
THA	12.6	7.6	10.5	3	2	13500	10500
65	11.7	11.7	8.6	3.79	1.72	9700	5200
TH1	9.6	5.8	9.3	3	2	12500	8500
THB	9.1	5.5	9	3	2	12000	7500
50	9	9	6.6	3.45	1.34	9700	5200
TH2	7.8	4.7	8.4	3	2	10500	7000
40	7.2	7.2	5.2	3.45	1.1	9700	5200

Table 1.4 Dry stresses for European oak, BS 5268 and CP112 combined.

sensible approach in this situation is to use the CP112 grades and grade stresses, using the method of grading specified therein, and it is instructive to compare these with present strength classes. Because the largest number of GS grades for softwoods is now found within C16, the associated allowable stresses are a sensible basis for design in structural timber. However, it may be unreasonable to assume the same strength class for existing timbers, and there is good reason to assume a higher grade.

The sensible timber to consider is *Pinus sylvestris* (Scots pine), and CP112 grades of this are compared with those in BS 5268 (Table 1.5), with the modern grades shown in bold type. SS grade, whose stresses are the equivalent of C24, lies between the old 50 and 65 grades; but, like oak, the modulus of elasticity values have improved. However, the possibility of grading timbers by the earlier method is not officially recognised, although the surface appearance of knots is all that one will normally have for timbers *in situ*. No work has been done to determine the most common grades found in buildings of this period, but, if their load-carrying capacity is not to be underestimated, C24 stresses are probably the most commonly applicable. The same is true of 19th century structures, when supplies began to come from North American forests. Timbers in buildings of this age tend to be larger than those in common use today, with knots that are smaller in proportion to the overall cross-section, so that a reasonably high grade should be achievable.

The strength of a member

The problem for the conservator is that the methods of determining timber strengths used in codes of practice have been devised to suit modern practice, and we have to make the best that we can with what we have. It may be that the modern codes are unduly conservative when applied to a structure that has been in service for some time and has shown no signs of distress. In such circumstances it would seem foolish to condemn the structure just because it does not conform to the norms of modern design practice; the successful performance of a standing structure is a better guide to its adequacy than any code of practice. Therefore, it is worth considering the level of safety provided by the modern codes. The structure being considered might also have a history of loading that produced stresses that exceeded those permitted by the grading rules. Evidence of this may then be used to justify proposed levels of stress in a repaired structure.

Grade	Bending and tension (N/mm²)	Compression, parallel (N/mm²)	Compression, perpendicular (N/mm²)	Shear, parallel (N/mm²)	E, mean (N/mm²)	E, min (N/mm²)
Basic	15.2	11.7	2.48	1.52	9700	5500
75	9.7	7.9	2.21	1.14	9700	5500
65	7.9	6.6	2.21	0.97	9700	7200
C24	**7.5**	**7.9**	**2.4**	**0.71**	**10800**	**7200**
C22	**6.8**	**7.5**	**2.3**	**0.71**	**9700**	**6500**
50	6.2	4.8	1.93	0.76	9700	5500
C18	**5.8**	**7.1**	**2.2**	**0.67**	**9100**	**6000**
C16	**5.3**	**6.8**	**2.2**	**0.67**	**8800**	**5800**
40	5.2	3.8	1.93	0.62	9700	5500

Table 1.5 Stresses for Pinus sylvestris: *CP112 and BS 5268 combined.*

Even if there are apparent defects, a structure that has been standing for some time and whose use is to remain unchanged is adequate at some level, so that its repair need only aim to make a significant improvement in that level of adequacy. It is when it is moved or there is a change of use that one needs to justify it in the light of modern codes.

Some increase in allowable stress is permitted for members that share loads between them – members such as floor joists and roof rafters. This is because there is a higher probability that timbers will be above the minimum stress for the grade. However, the increase is only a modest 10%. Note also that the allowable stresses are given for dry timber, but this actually means timber at 18% moisture content, which might be appropriate to an open unheated structure. In fact, the majority of timbers in a building will be much drier than this 18% moisture content; 5% would be a reasonable estimate for an enclosed and heated building. Because the strength of timber is dependent upon moisture content, some allowance could be made for timbers whose moisture content in service is always below that value, and Lavers (1969) provides data on which such an adjustment might be made.

The grade of a piece of timber is determined by its weakest point. Assume that there is a knot cluster that reduces a piece of timber that would otherwise be THA or SS grade (depending upon whether it is oak or softwood) to THB of GS grade and that this knot cluster occurs close to one end of the timber. If the piece is shortened by cutting off the knot cluster the result is a timber that would be graded to the higher grade. The example shows that the grade is not a constant for the whole length of a timber; it is simply assumed so because in most situations it is not known how the timber is to be used. The position in conservation work is rather different, because timbers are used more selectively. In a simply supported beam the bending stresses are highest at the centre of the span, so that the knot cluster assumed above will have the most severe effect if it occurs at that point. But if it occurs towards the end of the span, where the stresses are lower, it would be possible to assume the higher grade at the centre of the span, allowing the beam to carry a higher load.

Duration of load

The load-carrying capacity of timber is affected by the duration of the load. Timber can carry a larger load for a short period of time than it can

Duration of loading	Factor
Long term (e.g. dead + permanent imposed)	1.0
Medium term (e.g. dead + snow)	1.25
Short term (e.g. dead + imposed + wind)	1.5
Very short term (dead + imposed + wind)	1.75

Table 1.6 Modification factor for the duration of loading.

carry permanently.‡ Since many loads on structures are of short- or medium-term duration it follows that the timber may be able to sustain higher stresses resulting from these loads than the allowable long-term stresses. Therefore increases in stress for short- and medium-term loads are allowed in design, and the code of practice provides coefficients by which the long-term stresses may be multiplied (Table 1.6). In checking a structure it will normally be sensible to determine which of the various loads is critical: the permanent load acting alone or the permanent load in combination with a short- or medium-term load. Whether one treats the wind load as a short-term or very short-term load depends upon the size of the structure. The short-term load apples to structures where the largest dimension exceeds 50 m, and as the majority of historic timber structures are likely to be smaller than that the larger modification factor will be more frequently used.

Deflections

Deflections depend upon the modulus of elasticity and naturally this varies just as the strength does. The minimum modulus would be used when calculating the deflection of a single member acting alone: the main beam in a floor or a roof purlin, for example. The average modulus would be used for load-sharing members, such as rafters and floor joists. Because we are again working at either the bottom end or the bottom half of a distribution curve, the actual elastic deflection may well be less than that calculated. The difficulty is that there will be creep deflections added to these elastic deflections. Unfortunately, good data is not available for creep deflections over long periods of time when

---

‡ The load tests to determine the capacity of timbers are naturally of short duration, but the allowable design stresses derived from these are those that the timber will sustain permanently.

timbers have been loaded while still green, although we know that timbers like green oak can develop substantial deflections as they dry out.

Most of us will be familiar with the effect of creep. A simple bookshelf over a long span may have acceptable deflection when first loaded, but after a while can have a noticeably increased deflection. On removing the load (of books) it will be found to have a permanent set. This is the creep deflection that is in addition to the initial elastic deflection. Turn the shelf over and reload, and the set due to creep deflection and the present elastic deflection will now be in the opposite direction and (with luck) might cancel out, resulting in a horizontal shelf. However, any satisfaction at this happy result will be short-lived, because the shelf will again begin to creep under load. The creep does not continue forever, unless the stresses in the timber are a significant proportion of the ultimate stress, but is the effect that produces the shapes of roofs that we see where the purlin has sagged between the supporting frames. The extent of creep deflection is difficult to estimate because it depends upon the moisture content of the timber – it will be larger when moisture content is higher. We will need to return to the magnitude and effect of creep deflection in Chapter 4.

2

Basic timber structures

Just as the materials of construction divide into two types, the hard-woods and softwoods, so timber structures also divide into two types, roughly but not completely corresponding to the two types of materials. Timber framing formed the basic construction of the majority of buildings until the 17th century, after which masonry was used for external walls with internal timber structures. Oak, or some other hardwood, was used for timber-framed buildings, while softwoods were used for the timber structures in masonry buildings. It has already been noted that oak may have persisted in some areas and was preferred for some parts of the structure. At the same time, the timber framing tradition persisted in use for some buildings, with the frames being made of softwood: barns, for example. During the earlier period there were different framing methods in use and a variety of different carpentry traditions so that it is only possible to deal here with a small sample; naturally the most common.

The timber frame tradition

The variety of different timber frame traditions is seen in different structural arrangements, different patterns of wall framing and different roof framing. The most noticeable are the different types of wall framing. In England, close studding was used in some areas, square panels in others and elaborate chevron and quatrefoil bracing in the north and west of the country, and other traditions can be seen in other countries. For example, while the bracing of English timber frames is often by curved braces between posts and either wall plates or cills, German framing is often characterised by short, straight, steeply angled, intersecting braces. There is also a variation in roof types as well as in the supporting frames. The obvious division in roof types in England is between common rafter roofs and those relying upon purlins. The latter commonly have the purlins carried by a frame, or truss, although some houses, and certainly many churches, used arched structures as the basis for decorative roof forms. Later, flat lead roofs required beam structures, which in churches might also be decoratively treated. In Holland and Germany quite different types of roof with steep slopes are formed by structures that include two or more storeys of attic floors.

Of course, sloping roofs create outward thrusts, so that such roofs must either be buttressed or tied. Richard Harris (1989) has pointed out that English and continental framing differs in the tying of roofs. In English framing the tie beam is connected directly to the wall plate, resulting in a complex junction that includes the post (see Figure 3.12). In contrast, continental carpentry sets the tie beam into the post, thus avoiding this complication (Figure 2.1). This continental method has travelled across the Atlantic to the barn framing of America.

In England there is an obvious difference between cruck frame and box frame buildings, but Brunskill (1985) has divided English timber structures into three types: the cruck frame, the box frame and the post and stud frames. In this classification the last two differ only in the arrangement of studs and the framing of the roof. The box frame has

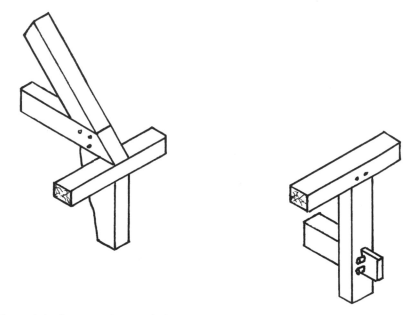

Figure 2.1 Comparative English and continental tie beams.

more widely spaced wall studs, commonly has bracing in the wall and carries a purlin roof (Figure 2.4). Brunskill's stud frame type has closely spaced wall studs without bracing in the wall and carries a common rafter roof. However, in many other respects their construction is similar and need not be distinguished. Both will be referred to here as box frame construction. To this list needs to be added aisled construction, because this type presents some structural issues that are different from the box frame to which it is related (Figure 2.5). While this distinguishes the main types of timber construction found in Britain, there are also variations within each that are too numerous to deal with here, but which have been described by a number of scholars (e.g. Mercer, 1975). It is sufficient to note that these variations in methods of framing, in the manner of bracing the frames and the kinds of roof structure, are often characteristic of particular regions. These variations will only be discussed here to the extent that they affect the structural behaviour.

Of course, the difficulty that faces conservators is that the buildings with which they are presented will seldom conform to the simple basic types. Even if dealing with an isolated rural building, later additions and adaptations of the original plan may well have involved changes to the basic frame. In urban locations the original property divisions may also have changed, so that the conservator can be looking at what was originally more than one building, at only part of a building, or possibly at a property that incorporates parts of two buildings where the remainder of each is in a different ownership. All of this is before one considers the changes that have taken place as the frames themselves have been altered to accommodate later needs (either changes in the internal planning or the arrangement of doors and windows) or have deteriorated. Therefore the first task of the conservator is to understand the history of the building, because that might have affected its structural integrity. This chapter can only offer the briefest guide to structural types to aid that process, but a little more information on this is provided in Chapter 8.

Cruck construction

Cruck construction is structurally the simplest form, comprising a series of transverse frames supporting wall plates and purlins. The distribution of cruck buildings is striking because it is restricted to Wales and the western half of England (Alcock, 1981). The frames comprise pairs of cruck blades that give the type its name, produced from long, curved timbers that give the desired shape, obtained from either a

Figure 2.2 Cruck frame.

curved trunk or from the trunk and main branch. Once hewn to a rect-angular cross-section, the timbers were then sawn down the middle to produce the matching pairs of blades that comprise the main timbers of the frame. In the simplest construction these would be connected together at the top and then joined by a collar to produce an A-shaped frame that could be easily handled (Figure 2.2). The collar is essential for erection because the centre of gravity of a curved blade lies outside the line joining the feet to the apex, so that a simple pair of blades joined together would tend to fold up during rearing. There were a variety of ways in which the crucks were joined together at the apex, which have been catalogued by Alcock (1981). Many have short pieces joining the blades at the apex, presumably because it was not always possible to obtain crucks long enough to be fastened together directly.

The frames for a building were assembled on the ground over the sole plate that formed the base of the building and then successively reared into position. In doing this, the first two frames would need to

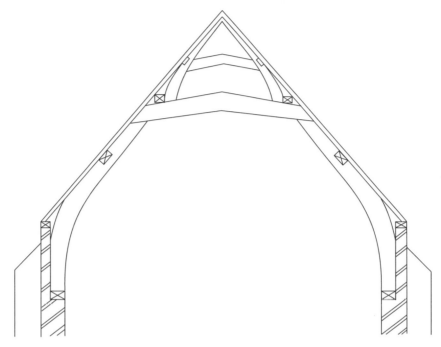

Figure 2.3 A raised base cruck. The frame for the upper part of the roof is a small cruck frame standing on the collar.

be temporarily propped until joined together with purlins and braced with wind braces. Once this stable structure was complete, successive frames could be reared and held in position by the next lengths of purlin. It will be apparent from this description that the timbers of the purlins were only one bay long and jointed at, or just beyond, each cruck frame. Short timbers, called cruck spurs, cantilevered from the cruck blades to support the wall plates, although it seems likely that the load was actually carried by the wall studs. The cruck spur might also support timbers that carried the purlins, because it was not always possible to obtain crucks of sufficient curvature for them to be able to support the purlins directly. Many of the joints used in cruck construction were lap joints. The wind braces were fastened to the cruck blades and the purlins with lap joints, and the cruck spur was sometimes fastened to the blade with a notched lap joint. This is probably because these joints were made to fit on site rather than being pre-cut in the workshop (the method used for box frame structures).

The largest cruck building that survives today is Leigh Court Barn, with a span approaching 35 ft (just over 10.5 m) (Horn and Charles,

1973), but it was not always possible to obtain such long crucks, the spans required often being larger than the timbers available. In such cases the tops of the cruck blades were joined by a long collar, with these three timbers braced together with knee braces to form each frame. This formed the so-called base cruck, which would then have a separate roof structure built above the collar (Figure 2.3). Base crucks were also used in association with aisled halls, where their use avoided the need for posts that would have obstructed the open space of the hall. Both normal crucks and base crucks were also raised off the ground in masonry walled buildings (as raised crucks or raised base crucks), but as the frames are arch-like structures, exerting an outward thrust, the masonry walls needed buttressing. Sometimes the roof above the collar was formed with another small cruck structure, as in a number of West Country barns (e.g. Glastonbury and Pilton), or the separate roof structure could be carried on separate tie beams set above the collar of the cruck frame, as in the monastic barn at Middle Littleton (Horn and Charles, 1966).

The box frame

The box frame is conceptually different from the cruck frame, and not just different in its method of construction. Although transverse frames can be identified within this type of building, it is essentially a load-bearing wall structure. Wall plates carry the weight of the roof, and these are carried by the framing of the walls beneath them. Moreover, the method of assembly is to frame the complete walls and to raise these into position, connecting them together with the transverse floor beams and roof tie beams. In a roof with trusses and purlins, the latter carry a proportion of the roof load back to the frames, but not sufficient load to make a clear distinction between this type of structure and that using only common rafters, as will be seen from Chapter 4. In framing box frame buildings the carpenter would mark up and make all the frames in the workshop prior to assembly on site. Consideration of this process shows that the building comprises frames in different planes (wall frames, floor frames and transverse frames), and that many of the timbers are components of more than one frame. For example, the main posts are part of either the front or rear wall as well as being part of a cross frame. Transverse floor beams, roof tie beams and principal rafters are part of the cross frames of the building as well as being part of the floor or roof. As the timbers were all scribed to fit those that they were

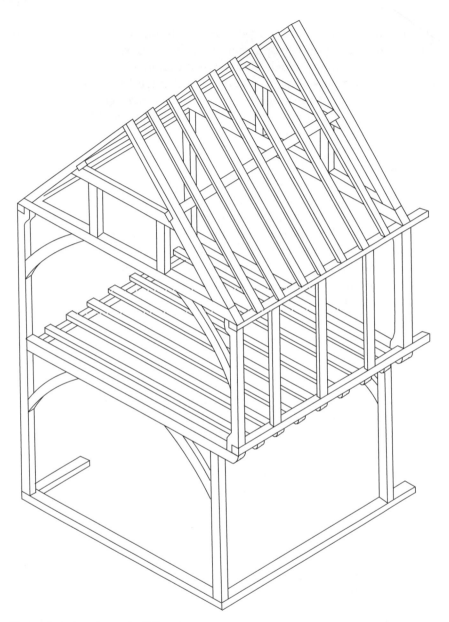

Figure 2.4 Box frame building.

framed into, the carpenter would have to set out each of these different frames in the workshop in order to mark up the timbers to fit each other. Thus each timber would be set up several times, and the same process is carried out today when timber frames are dismantled for repair.*

In medieval English framing two-storey buildings normally have a two-storey high rear wall frame, while a building with a jettied front would require two separate wall frames. In construction the rear wall frame and the ground floor wall at the front would be raised first and connected with the transverse floor beams, which would project over the head plate of the ground floor wall. As these transverse beams were put in place so would the spine beams of the floor and any ground floor braces to stabilise the structure. The floor joists could then be tenoned into the spine beam and pegged in place. This method of assembly requires that the joists sit on top of the top plates of the wall frame. With the framing of the floor complete the jetty sill, or bressummer, of the first floor wall could be placed and the first floor wall constructed on it, with the wall plates tied across the building by the roof tie beams. As at the ground floor, braces would need to be inserted as part of this operation. The completed box frame structure was then ready to receive the roof. Unless covered, joists had exposed end grain, and so were vulnerable to decay. In better quality buildings a moulded board would be used to cover these ends.

All the joints in the structure so far were mortice and tenon joints. Floor joists often have a bare-faced tenon at the bottom of the joists so that the mortices in the beam were close to the centre, where it would weaken the member the least (although whether this was recognised at the time is a moot point). At the other end the joists simply sat on the plate, allowing the floor at the front to be jettied beyond it. At the rear it would be a plate jointed into the posts. Because this plate was under the joists the mortice in the posts would be slightly lower than the mortice for the transverse beam, but with three mortices at nearly the same level for the intermediate posts in a frame this was still a considerable weakening.

---

* Although not part of the English timber frame tradition, it is worth noting that a quite different framing method was used in the North American colonies. There the framing method was to imagine an ideal rectangular section that lay inside each timber and to cut the joints to this. To do this, timbers need to be reduced at the joint to the dimensions of this ideal section. The effect of this is that, because it is unnecessary for timbers to be scribed to fit each other, the lengths of timbers between joints can be determined precisely without setting out each frame in the workshop.

Aisled frames

Most of the aisled frames that carpenters are likely to be involved in repairing today are in barns, although some domestic buildings used aisled construction (see Wood (1965) and Barnwell and Adams (1994)). This type of structure continued in use for agricultural buildings well into the era of softwood framing. Aisled frames normally comprised a pair of longitudinal frames, each consisting of arcade posts, arcade plate and longitudinal braces. These were joined together by tie beams and transverse braces (Figure 2.5), while aisle ties then joined the posts to the wall plates. That these were in tension was clearly recognised by the carpenters, because they are commonly jointed into the posts with

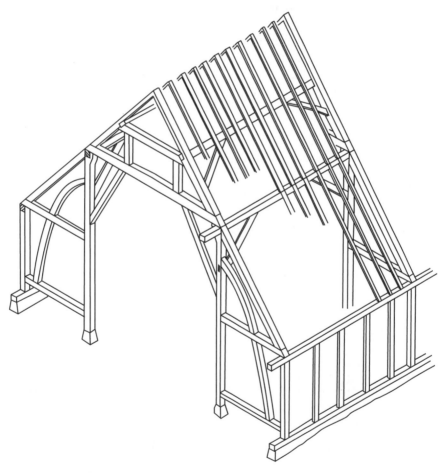

Figure 2.5 Aisled construction.

dovetail tenons, similar to the joint shown in Figure 3.15, but with a blind mortice. The walls could be separately framed in timber or built of masonry, the latter often replacing the former over time. With masonry walls the aisles can be open, i.e. with no timbers below the aisle ties, whereas in timber framed barns the aisle ties often form part of transverse aisle frames that also have a sole plate jointed into the wall. Transverse bracing could be provided with simple braces between posts and ties, but a common arrangement in buildings with timber-framed walls and aisle sole plates was to use 'passing braces' extending from the sole plate of the aisle framing across the aisle ties and into the back of the arcade posts as shown in Figure 2.5.

Roof types

Roofs are often the least altered part of the building, so their carpentry can sometimes be a good guide to the original construction of what has become a very different and possibly much more complex building below. The very wide variety of types that are found and their distributions have been discussed by such authors as Cordingley (1961) and Smith (1957). Although the taxonomies developed by these authors have to a large extent depended upon visual characteristics, while we are concerned with their structural behaviour, naturally there is a link between the two. The principal structural division is between common rafter roofs and purlin roofs. The simplest possible roof arrangement is a coupled rafter roof in which pairs of common rafters simply lean against each other. This would only be suitable for very small spans because rafters would sag under the weight of the covering, and therefore they have to be assisted in some way. Common rafter roofs normally have collar-braced rafters, the purpose of the collars being to reduce the bending on the rafters by strutting between them. The collars are therefore designed to be in compression. Common rafter roofs also include scissor-braced roofs (Figure 2.6) and those where the rafters are braced with soulaces and ashlar pieces.[†] These last types are important in larger span buildings with steeper pitched roofs, such as cathedrals, where scissor braces not only help to reduce rafter bending but are also important in carrying wind loads.

---

† Soulaces below the collar are joined to the rafters while vertical ashlar pieces, seen in Figure 2.6, strut the rafters from the inside face of the wall.

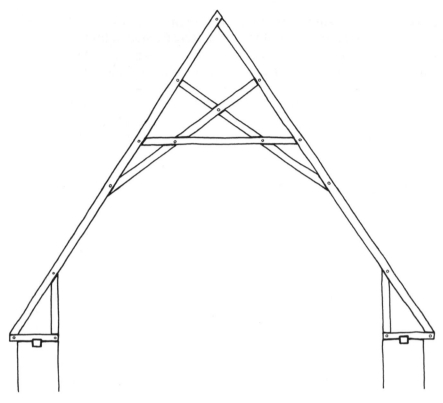

Figure 2.6 Scissors braced truss with a steep pitch. The type of roof found in churches and cathedrals.

Carpenters sometimes used crown posts and collar plates to give the roof longitudinal stability. Pairs of rafters, whether braced by a collar or not, are unstable, i.e. they will fall over unless held upright in some way. A restraining force can be provided by the timbering that supports the covering, battens for tiles, boarding for lead etc., although such restraint still requires something like a masonry gable wall to prevent the whole roof from racking. This racking of the roof can be seen in the high roofs of cathedrals for which restraining structures have sometimes been added in the past. Wren suggested a method for this at Salisbury Cathedral, which had suffered from racking, and additional structures were added at Westminster by Hawksmoor (McDowall *et al.*, 1966) and at Lincoln by James Essex (Foot *et al.*, 1986). Although various bracing methods have been tried, the most effective in these high roofs is to use diagonal boarding over the rafters when recovering them.

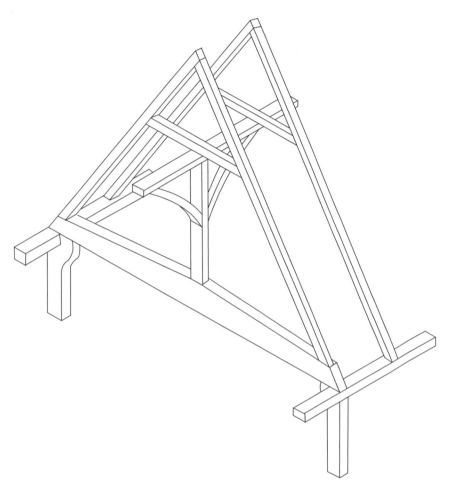

Figure 2.7 Crown post roof.

Many domestic buildings had crown post roofs to solve the problem of stability, an arrangement that could not be used conveniently in the higher roofs of cathedrals. A crown post is a post standing on the tie beam supporting a plate that runs under the collars, called a collar plate (Figure 2.7). (The term 'collar purlin' is also used, although this timber was not intended to carry load.) Bracing between the post and the collar plate provides longitudinal stability. Additionally, braces were sometimes provided between the post and the pair of rafters at that point or between the post and the tie beam. These would have aided assembly and ensured lateral stability of the post.

Purlin roofs

The alternative to bracing every pair of rafters is to introduce purlins to assist in carrying the load of the roof. Normally only one pair of purlins was used, placed halfway up the slope, but there might be two or even three pairs of purlins in very large-span roofs. The purlins must in turn be supported by some kind of roof frame, designed to carry load from the purlins to the walls or the posts of the building frame. Again a variety of arrangements was used, but many involved large 'principal rafters' to support the purlins that were then strutted in some way. Variations exist in both the way in which the purlins were jointed to the principal rafters and the way in which the latter were assisted by struts (Figure 2.8). The simplest carpentry has the purlins carried over the backs of the principals, which are notched to restrain them, but 'butt purlins' tenoned into the principals were common at one time. The mortices for these have the effect of weakening the principals at the point of maximum bending moment unless some strutting is provided there to assist them.

The principal rafters could simply be strutted across with a collar in much the same way as common rafters, but most relied upon some strutting from the tie beam. A commonly used arrangement has both collars and struts from the tie beam with the purlins resting on the collars (Figure 2.8(a)). This is called a clasped purlin roof because the purlins are clasped between collars and principal rafters. There are also arrangements in which the principal rafter is not called upon to receive the load from the purlins because they are strutted directly from the tie beam (see Chapter 4). Longitudinal stability of purlin roofs was ensured by 'wind bracing' between the purlins and principal rafters.

In purlin roofs there were also differences in the way in which the common rafters were supported. In some cases rafters spanned across the purlins, simply resting on them as they did so. Otherwise the rafters would be pegged to the purlins. The obvious structural significance of this is that the peg hole weakens the rafters at just the point of greatest bending moment. At their feet the rafters of medieval buildings are housed in sockets within the wall plate, with sprockets attached to their backs to continue tile support over the eaves. Of course, wind-driven rain may lodge within these sockets so that both rafter ends and wall plates are liable to decay.

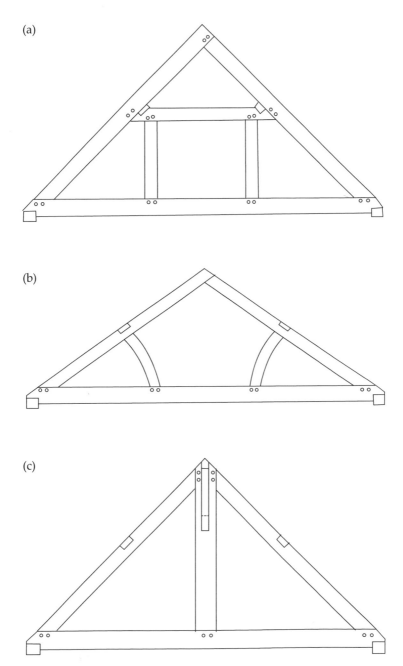

Figure 2.8 Types of purlin roof frames.

Construction and alterations

Because the frames were made in the workshop and then transported to site, the timbers had to be marked to identify their position in the building. A systematic numbering system was used so that these carpenter's marks provide a permanent indication of the sequence of construction (see Harris, 1989). The internal frames of medieval houses were built so that the good face of the timbers, the face from which the pegs were driven in, faced the upper end of the building, so that this was the face that the owner of the house saw when he dined, whereas the external frames face outwards. Thus one can determine the layout of the original house by an examination of the construction. The ability to recognise such features and to reconstruct the history of the building from such clues is not simply of antiquarian interest. Because later changes can involve both additions to the original frame or the subdivision of buildings, this may well have affected the integrity of the original structure. Thus the ability to understand the history of the building may well be important in understanding its structural behaviour and is often important in identifying the causes of structural distress. Such changes are discussed in Chapter 8.

The new carpentry

A new carpentry came into use during the 17th century which, during the 18th, gradually replaced the traditional forms described above. This was accompanied by the increasing use of softwood instead of oak for structural purposes and by a more significant change in building practice: the adoption of masonry for walls rather than timber framing. From then on houses comprised a masonry shell with timber floors and internal partitions, and an important function of the main floor timbers and the roof was to stabilise these walls. Floor framing arrangements changed, churches were built with galleries, and internal walls were trussed so that they could carry floors but also incorporate doorways. Thus, although the carpentry of buildings was less visible it was no less vital. The wall plate and tie beams were described by Palladio as 'a kind of ligament to the whole work'. This is a vital task, as some involved in the alteration of 18th century buildings have discovered to their cost; remove the internal timber and the external masonry walls may collapse.

The other clear purpose of the roof truss was to support the ceiling, as, by the 17th century, open roofs were already being abandoned in favour of plastered ceilings. This was not a trivial structural problem. Apart from the use of heavy lime plaster in domestic construction, which might be decoratively worked, vaulted ceilings were also used, especially in churches. These required timber falsework on which to fix the plaster laths, and all this had to be hung from the tie beam. Thus tie beam loads might be quite substantial. Once these new structural types had been introduced there were further developments: changes in the details of the carpentry, the introduction of new roof framing in the form of mansard roofs to provide increased accommodation, and eventually the more extensive adoption of queen-post trusses for roofs. Iron also became more extensively used in the framing of roof trusses.

Such changes made little difference to the framing of barns and other agricultural buildings, although the enclosures, and later improvements in agricultural methods, affected the distribution and the types of buildings put up. Industrial development also required new and larger building types with heavier floor loads and longer roof spans, and these developments would have stimulated changes in carpentry methods. It would, for example, have encouraged a change from king-post to queen-post roof trusses, required the use of longer and larger floor timbers, and presumably stimulated the introduction of iron in combination with timber. Of course this last development was to be given its greatest boost by the Industrial Revolution, which eventually led to the more general adoption of iron in both floor and roof structures.

These developments have been described in detail elsewhere (Yeomans, 1992a) but a brief review of the effect on carpentry detailing is worth considering. The most significant change was in the structural behaviour of roofs. No longer was the principal rafter supported by strutting from the tie beam; instead, struts were brought down to the base of posts that were in turn hung from the principal rafters. Thus posts were in tension rather than being in compression and the principal rafters acted like an arch, thrusting outwards on the ends of the tie beam. To cope with the transmission of forces iron strapping was introduced into the trusses.

These developments are also dealt with in contemporary carpenters' manuals, of which the most important are Price, Nicholson, Tredgold and Newlands. Francis Price (1733) produced the first, well-illustrated book on carpentry. It was comprehensive and above all the most accurate of the books appearing in the first half of the 18th century. Peter Nicholson, who first published in 1792, and Thomas Tredgold (1820) described the situation round the turn of the 19th century. A large number of titles were published in the name of Peter Nicholson, continuing till the mid-19th century, while Tredgold's work was revised and updated throughout the century. James Newlands (c1850) also provides a good account of carpentry at that time.

Floor structures

With the adoption of masonry construction instead of timber frames the layout of floors changed radically and beams tended to span at right angles to the main walls rather than parallel to them. The floor beams and joists were built into the masonry walls as construction proceeded, leaving the flooring to be added once the roof was on. This naked flooring as it was called both stabilised the walls and provided a working platform for the construction of the next storey. The simplest floors comprised common joists spanning between the main beams – although 'girders' was the term used at the time. In the better class of work there would be separate ceiling joists, so that the girders would not project into the room below. Also, in good quality construction pugging was added between the joists to act as a sound deadening material, but thereby increasing the load of the floor. A variety of materials were used: sand, sea-shells or even sawdust. This material required support from pugging boards set between the joists. The use of these then set the spacing of joists, as a board was 12 inches (305 mm) wide. Joist tenons now normally had haunches above the bearing of the tenon, providing a greater depth of timber to carry the shear force. Ceiling joists placed after construction of the rest of the floor would be fixed to the girders using pulley mortices: slots into which the joists could be slid. A possible layout of floor timbers in a house was shown by Price with double as well as single floors (Figure 2.9), the former marked Q and T in his plans and sections.

Double floors were used in good quality work. In these, binding joists, larger but less frequent than common joists, spanned between the girders. Over these were small bridging joists. The result is a stiffer floor (and rather difficult to analyse), but the intention was probably visual rather than structural. Both single and double floors can be found in the same house and on the same floor level, suggesting that the choice was simply so that the boards could be run in the desired direction. The position and thus direction of the girders would be determined by the stiffening needs of the walls, while the boards should run the length of the room. Clearly, if girders spanned the short direction in a large room the use of common joists required that the boards spanned the same way; double floors avoided this.

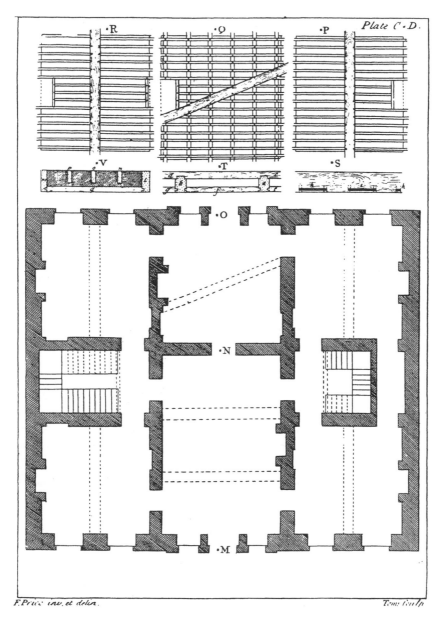

Figure 2.9 Examples of floor structures from Francis Price.

The sizes for floor joists and beams were first regulated in the Act for the rebuilding of London after the Great Fire. These distinguished between the sizes to be used for large buildings and those for small ones, presumably on the assumption that larger buildings should be of better quality and so have stiffer floors. The sizes stipulated by the Act were then reproduced in various texts, although authors began to give their own sizes. As fir was being imported as a substitute for oak these authors provided tables for both materials, although the basis of the sizes suggested is not known. Manuals (which differed from each other) at first recommended larger scantlings for the stronger oak, perhaps because it was the heavier material. Naturally floors in practice vary considerably, and one can find surprising differences in the sizes of timbers in adjacent buildings of the same size and built almost at the same time. This can probably be accounted for by vagaries in the supplies that carpenters could obtain.

Trussed girders were an important component of 18th century floors. These were used for long spans with the intention of increasing the strength of the member, although the trussing would have had little effect but to introduce some precamber into the beams (Dawes and Yeomans, 1985). The method was to cut the beam down the centre and then to cut matching chases into the two cut faces inclined upwards towards the centre (Figure 2.10). Pieces of 'hard timber', called 'trussing pieces' or simply 'trusses', were then placed in the chases and the whole beam reassembled with the two halves bolted together. Wedges were then driven into the space between the ends of the trusses to tighten them. In some arrangements three trussing pieces were used. Early girders used so-called dovetail pieces that were put in first and the wedges driven between them. Later, trussed girders used iron wedges and iron end stops (as seen in Figure 2.10). There are also instances of girders being trussed externally, although it would not have been as easy to frame in the floor joists.

Trussed girders are easily identified because the combined depth of the chases were not as great as the width of the trussing pieces so that the appearance is of a pair of beams close together between which the sloping top of the trusses can be seen. The bolts holding all this together can also

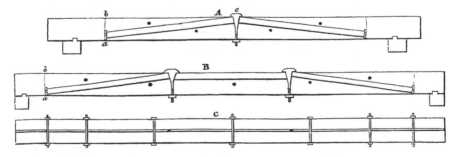

Figure 2.10 Trussed girders illustrated by Peter Nicholson.

be seen on the sides of the beams. While it is clear to us today that the removal of timber from the beam and its replacement with another piece of timber can produce no strength advantage, carpenters at the time were probably impressed by the upward spring in the beam as the wedges were driven in. It was not until Barlow's (1817) work that it was realised that there was no real advantage in the trussing of girders; nevertheless, structures using this device have generally been satisfactory.

Some scientific thinking over the sizes of structural members was attempted by both Nicholson and Tredgold, the authors of the most important early 19th century carpenters' manuals. (Barlow's more scientific work on the strength of timber was unlikely to have been read by carpenters.) They suggested formulae on which sizes might be based although they did not make clear the rationale behind these. By the end of the 19th century tables of sizes were being provided by some cities in their by-laws or building Acts although they were not a feature of the model by-laws that supplemented the Public Health Act governing building construction.

Roof carpentry

The most visible difference in the new roofs is of course the change in the pitch, and Francis Price (1733) showed how these were set out (Figure 2.11). The pitch was determined by making the height of the king post some division of the span. Price recommended three slopes to suit lead roofs, pantile roofs and slate roofs. The last was at 45° simply by making the length of the king post half the span. In the others the king post was 1/4 and 3/8 of the span (Figure 2.11). These correspond to angles of $\tan^{-1} 0.5$ and $\tan^{-1} 0.75$, i.e $26\frac{1}{2}°$ and 37° respectively. To the casual eye both of these might appear to be 30°, and for simplicity a slope of 30° will be assumed for the calculations in Chapter 6.

The detail that characterises the adoption of this type of roof structure in England is the use of joggled posts. While roofs with suspended king posts were used elsewhere in Europe, they all relied upon the compression members being let into the sides of the posts that they supported. This is true of roofs in Italy, our source in 17th century England of these new structural ideas, as well as in France and Germany. Why English carpenters chose to use joggled posts is not known, because this detail involves the use of larger timbers from which the posts are to be cut and more labour in execution. It does, however, make the behaviour of the structure very clear.

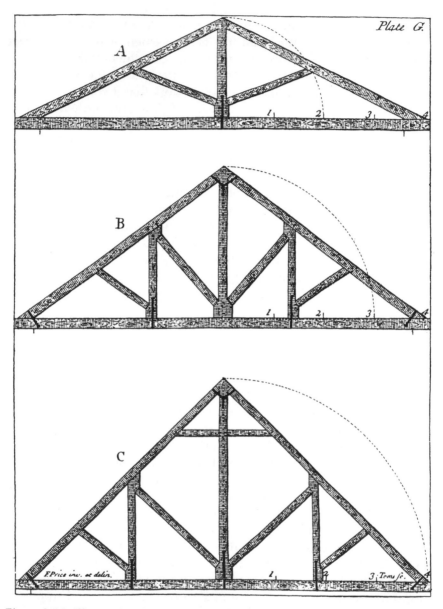

Figure 2.11 Illustrations by Francis Price showing the setting out of different roof pitches.

It is not certain how well the behaviour of the truss was understood until Nicholson, in 1792, described the working of a simple truss in qualitative terms. He describes something a little more complex than a basic king-post truss, with a pair of secondary posts and struts to carry

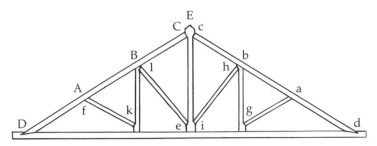

Figure 2.12 Diagram from Peter Nicholson used to explain the behaviour of a king-post roof truss.

two pairs of purlins (Figure 2.12). If one is not put off by his rather old fashioned nomenclature and use of English, this description is a model of clarity:

Let the two rafters CD, and cd, be firmly fixed to the tie beam Dd, and the upper ends Cc, be fixed to the king post E, the joggles being at right angles to the rafters. It is evident that if a weight acts upon the point E, the vertex of the truss, it will not descend; for suppose the rafters to revolve at the points D, d, to descent, the points C, c must come nearer to each other; but this cannot be so long as the top of the king post is incompressible, and therefore neither the king-post nor the rafters can descend. Instead of a weight acting at E, suppose a weight hung or suspended there, acting in the direction of the king-post E, e; a weight thus suspended will endeavour to make the king post descend, the same as when acting at E, now in the endeavour of the king-post to descend, it must force upon the rafters CD and cd; but as these are fast at their buttments or points D d, the force which acts at the points C, c will push the rafters in the direction of CD and cd, consequently the force of the thrust will terminate on the tie beam at the points D, d, and will endeavour to extend the beam. Wherefore if this truss should fail, the rafters must burst, and the tie-beam broken by the tension.

Now if the roof has purlins which stand upon the points A, B, a, b, a force acting on these points will clearly bend the rafters. wherefore it will be necessary to find some fixed points in order to keep the points A, B, a, b, from descending or in other words to prevent the rafters bending. To this purpose, fix the side posts l k and h g, under the purlins B b and also put in the braces l e, h i, so that the buttments at l, e, i, h, may be at right angles to the direction of the braces; then the points B, b, cannot descend, for they are supported by the points e, i, on the king post, which was shown to be immovable, and therefore the points B, b, will also be immovable: further the shoulders at l and h will prevent the side post l k and b g descending and consequently if the braces f k and g k, are placed under the points A and a, and are firmly fixed at the bottom of the posts l k and b g, the points A and a will also be supported.

Trusses were normally spaced at 10 ft (3 m) centres, and although they commonly supported a roof of purlins and common rafters, some early roofs used closely spaced purlins between the principal rafters, i.e. without common rafters. This may have been convenient for supporting boarding that was even used for slate as well as lead roofs. In many cases this early arrangement has been altered in later re-roofing work and replaced with large purlins and common rafters. Evidence of the early arrangement is seen in empty mortices in the principals. (Of course a change of mind during construction is also possible, because some contracts specify one arrangement although it was the other that was actually built.) An illustration by Nicholson (Figure 2.13) shows a

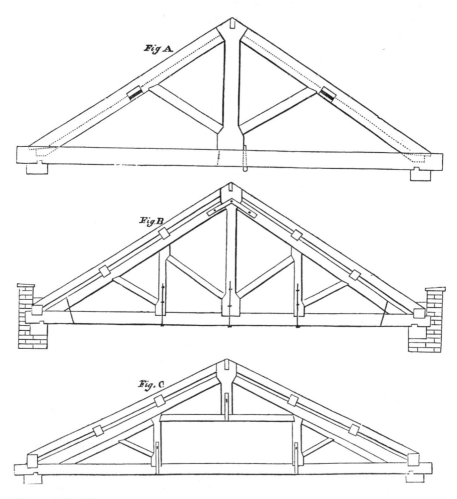

Figure 2.13 King-post and queen-post roof trusses illustrated by Peter Nicholson.

basic king-post truss, the development with secondary posts and a queen-post truss. Early trussed roofs had purlins tenoned into the principal rafters (as seen in Nicholson's basic king-post truss), but later in the 18th century a simpler arrangement came into common use in which purlins were carried on the backs of the principals. A block of timber was often fixed to the principals below the purlins to hold them in position, although Nicholson shows them trenched in. With this arrangement it was not possible to bring the common rafters down to the wall plate, so an additional plate, called a pole plate, was added across the top of the tie beam ends to receive the ends of the rafters. At the top, common rafters were simply butted against a ridge board.

One sometimes sees purlins that are set vertically rather than orthogonal to the pitch of the roof and tenoned through the principal rafters (Figure 2.14). With this arrangement the forces on the purlin comprise both a horizontal and a vertical load from the upper rafters, while the lower rafters only obtain horizontal 'support' from the purlin. Of course, as the upper and lower rafters are likely to be of the same length, the horizontal force from the former is the same as that from the latter. The result is that the purlin will simply be carrying a vertical load equal to the weight of the upper slope.

Until the introduction of trussed roofs the tie beam was the longest timber needed. Now, with limited bending moments on the beam it could be made in two halves. The joint between them was originally with a splayed, tabled scarf joint tightened by a wedge at the centre. Scarf joints were also made with iron bolts to both hold the timbers

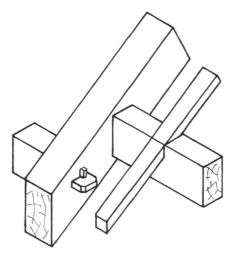

Figure 2.14 Purlins set vertically.

together and transmit the tensile force. Iron straps might also be used across the joint between the two halves of the tie. Simple, side-by-side scarf joints for tie beams with bolts to fasten them together eventually came into use later in the 18th century.

The tie beam needed support from the king post, and this was first done using a metal strap from the bottom of the king post round the tie beam. This was there to 'truss up' and so support the tie that was carrying the ceiling load. Because the tie beam was commonly wider than the post the strap was (in the best work) let through slots in the tie and was then fastened to the post with one or two bolts (Figure 2.15). These were at first forelock bolts, but after the first couple of decades of the 18th century bolts with nuts were increasingly used. An alternative early fixing was to use a half dovetail at the foot of the king post that was held into the tie beam mortice with a wedge (as seen in Nicholson's basic king-post truss: Figures 2.13 and 3.15). More sophisticated fasteners used in the 19th century are discussed later.

The critical heel joint at the foot of the principal rafters at first remained the same as that used previously: a simple mortice and tenon joint. Wren, Hawksmoor and Gibbs are known to have designed trusses in which the principal rafter butted against an iron strap that was then bolted down to the tie beam, suggesting an unwillingness to rely on carpentry for this joint. However, such examples are rare. Eventually notches in the tie beam were introduced to receive thrusts from the principal rafter, and bridle joints also came into use, superseding the

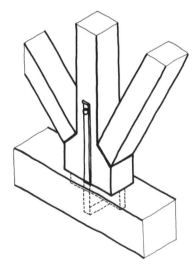

Figure 2.15 Metal strap at the foot of the king post.

mortice and tenon joints. These were by then routinely fastened with a stitch bolt, i.e. a bolt through both the tie and principal rafter fastening them together.

The king-post truss is a very robust structure, i.e. it will accommodate a wide range of spans and accept considerable variation in carpentry details without signs of distress. Nevertheless, as spans increased, secondary posts and struts were often added to provide additional support to the tie beam and help the principals to carry a second pair of purlins. The form was also modified to provide trusses with raised tie beams, used for example in 18th century churches that had shallow vaulted ceilings rising above the wall plate. This required the tie beams to be part-way up the principal rafters. In these trusses additional members were bolted close to the centre of the raised tie and rested on the wall plate with the principal rafters set on top of them. That they were below the principals at the wall plate leaves no doubt that they were designed to be in tension, but restraint against outward movement of the plate must have been provided by both these and by some bending in principals. The raised tie was therefore strapped to the principals, so that the whole truss relied upon a number of bolted fastenings.

Queen-post trusses

In the 17th and early 18th century, queen-post trusses were used to provide long spanning roofs with flat tops, an arrangement that provided the appearance of a steeply sloping roof but limited its height (Figure 2.16, top). Towards the end of the 18th century, queen-post trusses became increasingly popular for simple ridge roofs because by dividing the span into thirds rather than in half they provided two points of support to the tie beam and, with a pair of struts, provided for two pairs of purlins (Figure 2.13). These trusses also required shorter lengths of timber for the same span. Another advantage of queen-post trusses is that they provided usable space inside the roof. This might have been used to provide an attic floor, but it is also possible to consider introducing one today. If so an increase in the load on the roof will need to be considered.

There were several ways of arranging to have a simple ridged roof carried by a queen-post truss. Those described by Price had the tops of the queen posts tenoned into long principal rafters. A more normal

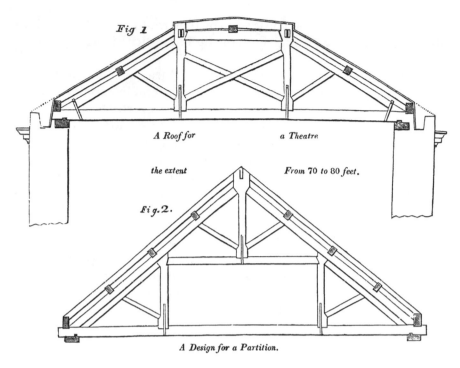

Figure 2.16 Queen-post arrangements.

arrangement, and the kind of framing that he used himself when he re-roofed Salisbury Cathedral, is to have short principal rafters strutting under a joggle at the head of the queen post. A continuous rafter is then laid over the top of this principal to form the roof slope. The basic framing is thus like that used for forming flat-topped roofs. Of course, it was still possible for the queen posts to be tenoned into this long rafter and that was certainly done, but it would have been to locate it rather than transmit any load. In yet another commonly found arrangement a separate king post stands on the straining beam (Figure 2.16, bottom). This might be framed into the long principals (as shown) or into short principals above the head of the queen posts. Variations on this may have a single horizontal timber between the heads of the queen-posts, so that the straining beam of the queen-post truss is also the tie beam of the king-post truss above it, or there may be two separate horizontal timbers, the straining beam and the tie beam.

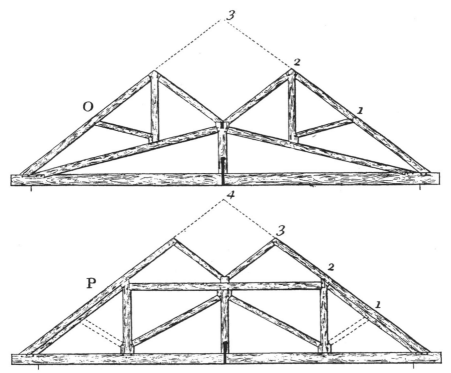

Figure 2.17 M shaped roofs illustrated by Francis Price using both king- and queen-post trusses.

Other roof forms

Both king-post and queen-post roofs were used in a variety of roof forms that conservators may well have to deal with. Short-spanning trusses might be used in combination with beams supported on the heads of posts to form flat-topped roofs with lead covers. Some deep plan buildings have simple king-post trussed roofs round the perimeter draining to lead-roofed wells in the centre. Urban houses might use trusses to support quite low roofs, designed to be hidden behind parapets but with sufficient slope to allow slates to be used rather than the more expensive lead. Price provides examples of this using both king- and queen-post trusses (Figure 2.17).

The other common urban form is the mansard roof incorporating attic rooms. The basic arrangement here is for inclined members forming the lower slope of the mansard to support a plate on which the upper part of the roof stands. There a variety of structural arrangements can be used to support the upper slope. In contrast, some 18th century urban houses had the roofs hidden as far as was possible behind a parapet. A far more common system for London terraced houses had a beam running from front to back of the house with a pair of hips to the chimney stacks either side.

The introduction of box gutters and lead flats within roofs made these roofs vulnerable to decay. Failure of the lead of either the gutter or the roof flat might go unnoticed until considerable damage had occurred to the timbers as a result of penetrating water and consequent decay. Thus a common repair that is needed is the replacement of tie beam and principal rafter ends.

Laminated timber was developed and used for roof construction in the mid-19th century and this needs to be mentioned for the sake of completeness, even though its repair will not be dealt with. There are two types of laminated timber, the older one used in Britain deriving from the ideas of Philipe de l'Orme (1561). This used boards cut to a curve and assembled side by side to form timber arches. This kind of construction was known here in the 17th century and used by Wren, and it was the method used for the arched transept roof of the Crystal Palace. The other method involves fastening boards one above the other and curving them to form the arch. The boards might be glued or nailed together. The original arches of Kings Cross Station were made in this way, and the nearby German Gymnasium, with similar laminated arches and built shortly after, still survives. It seems to have been a widely used method for long span roofs, used, for example, for drill halls. A number of woollen mills in Yorkshire had roofs like this and Manchester had snooker halls and swimming pools built with this type of roof.

Internal partitions

Early books on building suggest that timber partitions, i.e. internal walls, were used in preference to brick walls simply because they were cheaper. However, they could also be designed to be self-supporting between the masonry walls, so that walls on upper floors did not have to be supported by walls on the lower floors, enabling the plan to vary from floor to floor. This was done by trussing the partitions using either king-post or queen-post truss forms (Figure 2.18). Such trussed partitions might also be used to support floor timbers. At first these trussed partitions were just of timber, but later trusses were built with iron tie rods used to support the lower plate of the partition, transmitting load

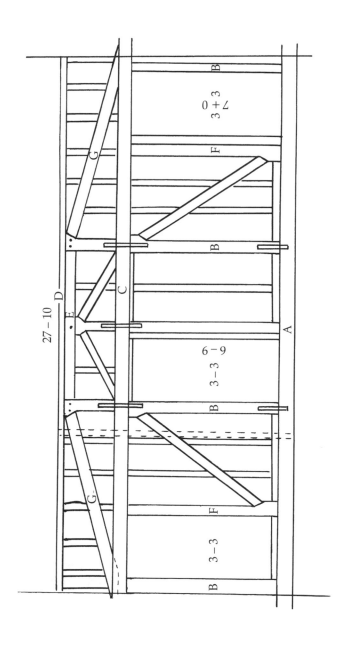

Figure 2.18 A trussed partition.

to the top plate and thus into the timber trussing. These tie rods would commonly be parallelled by a timber post.

Trussing in some cases involved the whole of the depth of the wall from floor to floor. It was still possible to have openings through such partitions, providing that a queen-post arrangement was used and the doorway was between the two posts. Greater flexibility in the positioning of the doorways was possible by having the trussing confined to the zone between the head of the door (or doors) and the floor above. In such cases long tie members would be required to support the floor below, and these would have to be attached to the truss with metal straps or eventually by tie rods.

The difficulty faced by the conservator is that the nature of the trussing in these partitions might not be known without removal of the covering lath and plaster, although some non-destructive methods such as thermal imaging are available. It can also be a source of structural problems because alterations to buildings of this period might involve the cutting of new doorways, and examples have been found where this work has cut through the structural elements of such partitions. Unfortunately the presence of tie rods has not always inhibited such alterations, and they may well have been cut through, just as were the timber posts.

Ironwork

By the end of the century, the passive strap between the king post and the tie beam, which would not take up load without some initial deflection of the tie beam, was replaced by more active devices that could be tightened up during construction (see Chapter 3). At the heel joint there was some concern about the security of the mortice and tenon joint. Roger Pratt noted that the feet of the principals 'be very strongly footed, bolted and keyed to prevent the kicking of them up' (Gunther, 1928: 212). Thus would account for the use of metal strapping or stitch bolts to fix the principal rafters to the tie beam. The other place where strapping was used was at the head of the king post, but the purpose of this is a little difficult to understand. Peter Nicholson (1792) suggested that its purpose was to overcome problems of shrinkage, noting that:

> As wood is more apt to shrink sideways than in length, so the king post and side posts in consequence of the perpendicular position of the grain in the wood, and also in proportion to the quality of the

wood, will be liable to shrink, the rafters of consequence will descend; this must be guarded against by the application of iron straps in proper positions...

However, it is a little difficult to imagine that any such strap could have carried the necessary forces. This certainly could not have been the intention behind the Y-shaped straps that Hawksmoor used, which went over the top of the principal rafters and down the king post. Their purpose seems to have been to prevent the ends of the principals from sliding up the joggles, which were not made perpendicular to the rafters as Nicholson recommends. Thus they were fulfilling a duty similar to that of the strapping at the heel joint.

Iron rods from which floor timbers were hung were used by architects as early as Wren, but came into more common use in the late 18th century, when (as noted above) they were incorporated into trussed partitions. This was part of the more general and gradual replacement of carpentry by iron components in the 19th century, with iron rods used for the tension members of trusses and castings used for making connections instead of carpentry (Yeomans, 1992a). A very early use of such a device was in the Porter Tunn Room roof at Whitbread Brewery. For this, a pair of castings were attached to the top of the king post to receive the ends of the principals. The fixing for each of these was just six comparatively small wood screws, the load in which must have well exceeded that allowed by the current code of practice.

Eventually the use of timber ties and metal strapping was superseded by using iron tie rods for the torsion members. Their use also enabled a range of new truss forms to be devised, because a straight timber tie beam was no longer required. Long timber principal rafters were strutted with short timbers trussed with wrought iron rods with the assembly completed with iron castings.

3

The form and behaviour of historic joints

At this stage it is appropriate to make some general comments on joints, because the behaviour of these normally governs the capacity of the structure. This chapter deals with the joints that will be found in existing carpentry, while modern timber fasteners and the types of joint associated with these will be dealt with in Chapter 7. The most important joint is the mortice and tenon because of its almost universal use, but the lap dovetail was used in the connection of the roof to the walls, while the behaviour of scarf and bridle joints may also be significant. In general it is the behaviour of joints under compressive loads that is our primary concern, but, when looking at the overall behaviour of a frame, the engineer may be concerned about its racking and the ability of the joints to transmit bending moments. Also, mortice and tenon joints in braces designed to carry wind loads may be called upon to act in tension. Of course there are no reliable methods of analysis that can be applied to the behaviour of pegged joints, even if we could guarantee the soundness of the pegs – which we cannot. And the position is little better for the metal bolts used for later softwood structures. Certainly they lie outside the range of data provided for modern metal fasteners.

Mortice and tenon

Mortice and tenon joints in oak-framed structures were put together with pegs. By boring the holes for the pegs in the tenon and the mortice slightly out of line, the effect of driving in the peg was to draw the timbers together so that the joint was made tight – a process called 'draw boring'. This would have introduced some pre-compression in the joint, but by an unknown amount, and some bending in the peg. The effect is that a joint that is fairly loose when it is put together becomes tight once the pegs are driven in, and it is not hard to see why. The pegs draw the shoulders of the tenon tight against those of the mortice. Although subsequent deterioration of the timbers may well have eliminated this pre-compression in some joints, it is useful to consider how such joints may behave when assembled in this way, and to do so we have to examine the behaviour of the pegs.

Figure 3.1(a) shows the forces on both the peg and the mortice and tenon for a simple situation in which the joint is in the centre of the morticed piece (called here the foundation member). The peg is pushing in one direction on the tenon in the attached member and in the other on the holes through the foundation member (Figure 3.1(a)). These forces must be equal, but the latter are not themselves equal because the pegs are tapered. This means that the force will be greater toward the head of the peg. In practice the joint is commonly offset toward this side of the timber, further increasing the stresses so that any splitting of the timber beside the mortice will occur on that side. Once the joint is tight, the timber at the side of the mortice will be put into compression between the edge of the hole and the shoulder of the foundation member (Figure 3.1(b)). The issue here is what is known as edge distance in modern fasteners, although the fastener is made of the

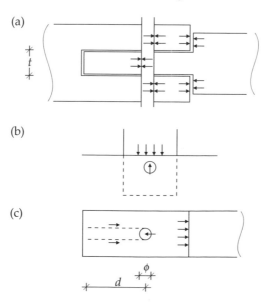

Figure 3.1 Forces in a pegged joint.

same material as the frame rather than of steel. Because the timber is in compression between these two forces the practical effect should be that the peg hole could be very close to the edge of the member – the shoulder of the tenon is 'supporting' the timber next to the hole. Failure can only occur if there is shrinkage of the timber so that the joint is no longer tight, i.e. there is no pressure on the shoulder of the mortice, while at the same time there is pressure from the pegs on the sides of the hole. In such circumstances one would expect to see splitting along the grain from the centre of the peg hole. In practice it is not always as simple as this. If the hole is too close to the edge, driving the peg in can cause a fracture across the narrow bridge of timber over the hole.

If there is enough timber in the foundation member then the tenon alone can be considered. There are now three possible modes of failure: crushing of the peg, shear failure of the peg and shear failure of the tenon (Figure 3.1(c)). These three can be compared using the allowable stresses in BS 5268, although they are not directly applicable to this situation. By using the relationship between the various allowable stresses, a rather simplistic idea can be obtained for critical dimensions of the joint (see Appendix 3). This suggests that the length to the end of the timber needs to be equal to or greater than the diameter of the peg if crushing of the peg is to occur before shear failure of the timber in the tenon. The difficulty is that the peg will almost certainly crush to some extent, as evidenced by those that have been recovered from joints. However, it has nowhere to go, so this simply results in higher loads on the sides of the hole so that shear failure of the tenon is a distinct possibility. Although this is not uncommon, where joints have failed in this way there has usually been some wetting of the timber. Shear failure across the peg might be compared with shear failure of the tenon, but the relationship is more complex because the required end distance suggested is related to the diameter of the peg and the thickness of the tenon. We also have no idea how shear strength of the peg might be modified by bending and compression beyond its elastic limit.

Tenons in braces

When two members are framed together at right angles to each other it seems obvious that the tenon will be the full width of the member on which it is formed. However, when members are at an angle to each other, what would be obvious to a carpenter who has to make joints is clearly not obvious to some professionals who survey structures. The joints are not easy to inspect, and some of the assumptions made about the form of the tenon seen in some drawings are impractical. Where the members are at an angle, the tenon will still be the full width of the member, but neither the tenon nor the mortice will be undercut. Undercutting the tenon would leave short-grain timber that would tend to break off, while undercutting the mortice would result in a joint that is rather difficult to assemble. Therefore the form that should be assumed is as Figure 3.2. This will be the case in both oak frames and later softwood roof trusses.

Recognising the shape of this mortice is important in surveying structures because one often finds empty mortice holes. If the mortice has square cut ends then the timber framed into it was at right angles to it. A mortice with a sloping end will indicate a brace and the angle of that brace to the member. Sometimes this indicates a missing brace, sometimes simply a reused piece of timber. The exception to this is where tenons take the form of half dovetails with the express purpose of resisting tensile forces. These are seen in some king-post roofs and in aisle ties: sometimes open, as in Figure 3.15, and sometimes with blind mortices.

In simple compression

If the member with the tenon is in simple compression then the load will be transmitted across the shoulders of the joint. This is the situation where studs tenon into horizontal plates. The critical stress will be the compression across the grain in the morticed member. In cases where

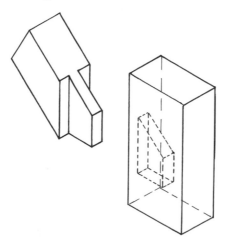

Figure 3.2 The shape of tenon used for an inclined brace.

members are at an angle there are two components of the compression force to be considered: that across the shoulder of the joint and that between the end of the tenon and the back of the mortice. The latter will normally be critical, as the two components will be similar but the area in compression is much smaller (the dark shaded areas in Figure 3.3(a)). Also the load is applied at an angle to the grain, and for such cases Hankinson's formula needs to be applied to determine the allowable stress (see Appendix 4).

In the joint at the end of principal rafters there is also the short grain in the timber behind the mortice to consider. This carries the outward thrust from the principal rafter in shear parallel to the grain. Figure 3.3(b) shows the area of timber behind the mortice that is resisting shear. Failures some-times seen here are probably as a result of weakening of the timber through the wetting of what is a relatively exposed joint so that the timber fails at a lower shear stress than normal. While the code of practice pro-vides a modification factor for the allowable stresses for timber in exposed conditions (service class 3), of concern here might be the reduction of strength because of decay occasioned by long-term wetting.

When considering the shear behind the mortice (as in Figure 3.3(b)) there is the question of whether or not it is sensible to take the average shear stress on the areas shown. This has been the practice of the author, but BS 5268 offers no guidance on this. A comparable situation occurs with the loaded end distance for split ring connectors. Here STEP1,

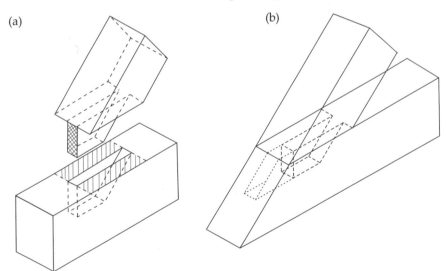

Figure 3.3 Heel joint showing: (a) bearing surfaces to take the horizontal and ver-tical components of the rafter thrust; (b) the area behind the mortice loaded in shear parallel to the grain.

Chapter C9 provides a means of calculating the characteristic load, which gives a comparable result to that dervied from allowable stresses.

In shear

Tenons on the ends of joists or beams carry the load in shear. A tenon on the end of a joist or a beam is shallower than the member it is supporting and this will limit the shear that can be transmitted by the member. Early joists often had simple bare-faced tenons at their ends (Figure 3.4(a)) effectively forming a notched end support, so the rules given in the code of practice for this condition might be applied to the load-carrying capacity. For a notch cut above the bearing a higher shear stress may be allowed on the tenon (Figure 3.5)

The factor K_5 by which the stress may be increased is given by:

$$K_5 = h(h_e - a) + a h_e / h_e^2$$

providing that $h_e > a$.

It can be seen from this that where $a = 0$ the shear strength of the full section is developed, but this is reduced when the tenon pulls out of the

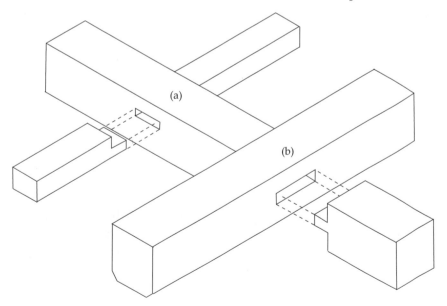

Figure 3.4 Floor joist tenon (top) and tenon between spine beam and transverse beam (bottom).

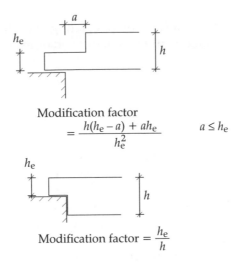

Modification factor

$$= \frac{h(h_e - a) + ah_e}{h_e^2} \qquad a \leq h_e$$

Modification factor $= \dfrac{h_e}{h}$

Figure 3.5 Notched bearings from BS 5268.

mortice, as so often occurs because of shrinkage of the beam. However, there is also a limit on the depth of the notch, which must not be greater than half the depth of the beam. Unfortunately tenons in floor joists are much shallower than this and, in the absence of any other guidance, it may be assumed that the limit on the depth of the notch effectively provides a limit on the value of K_5 which may not be greater than 2. This would apply if the joist were only twice the depth of the tenon, so if the joint is tight this factor could be used.

Shear is seldom a problem for joists because stresses are generally low and less of a problem for later joists, where haunched tenons were used that provided a greater depth of timber to carry the shear. However, it may be a problem for spine beams tenoned into transverse beams, where shear forces are much higher and the tenon is insufficient to carry the load without some enhancement of allowable stress. Here tenons are also usually part-way up the beam (Figure 3.4(b)) and one might well assume the rule for notches below the support. In this case K_5 is less than 1 to limit splitting at the root of the notch and if the code of practice rules are strictly applied, they could reduce the apparent strength to zero, especially as these tenons also contravene the rule that the notch may not be more than half the depth of the beam. Of course, there is material above and behind the tenon, and since this clearly contributes to the strength we could take this into account, effectively ignoring material below the soffit of the tenon. This seems to be a sensible approach. Joints like this in oak frames have a

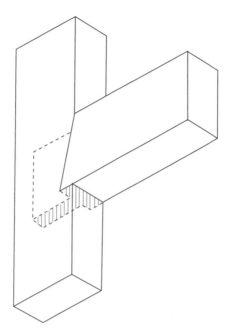

Figure 3.6 Notch to increase capacity of mortice and tenon loaded at right angles to the grain.

long history of loading and failures are seldom seen. We might also note that the rules in the code of practice have been drawn up with modern softwood structures in mind rather than oak.

Tenons can be loaded with a shear load on the narrow face of the tenon. This occurs where the main transverse floor beam is tenoned into the rear post of the frame (Figure 3.6), or where a collar is tenoned into principal rafters (see Figure 4.10(b)). A similar detail was also used in later roof trusses, where posts tenon into principal rafters or tie and have an inclined brace bearing against them. While such tenons might be very heavily loaded some are plain mortice and tenon joints, but others have the added sophistication of this notch to carry the load. The beam of Figure 3.6 is also often assisted by a brace between post and beam.

Joints in tension and moments on joints

The braces in a frame member may be in either compression or tension depending upon the direction of the externally applied load. For members to act in tension the load to them must be transmitted by the fixing pegs. Because of the issues discussed earlier a conservative approach is to assume that all braces act in compression only. (This is even true for so-called tension braces used in the walls of some framing traditions.) If this assumption is made the structure being analysed may well be different in different directions of loading. This becomes important in the consideration of wind loads in Chapter 4.

Braces in a frame are commonly at about 45° to the member into which they are framed. However, cruck frames and collar-braced principal rafters have long curved braces that are at a shallow angle to both collar and either cruck blade or principal rafter, with a correspondingly long tenon (Figure 3.7). Here the grain is at a very shallow angle to the line of the tenon and the pegs will be applying forces almost perpendicular to the grain. However, such joints also have a larger number of pegs, thus reducing the load that each might be carrying. While one might therefore assume that the joint is able to carry some tensile force, the joint often fails in the tenon by splitting between the peg holes. Observation suggests that this more commonly occurs in the tenon into the collar rather than into the principal rafter (or cruck blade), possibly because this is the shorter tenon with larger loads on each peg. Therefore, for wind load calculations in the next chapter it has still been assumed that such braces act in compression only.

The other situation in which the pegs may be called upon to resist tension is in a rectangular frame resisting racking load in the plane of the wall. Consider the effect of loading a pegged mortice and tenon joint in bending, the joint assumed to be fixed with two pegs (Figure 3.8). At one end of the joint there will be compression forces between

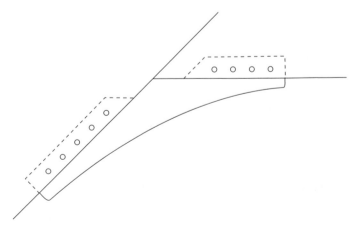

Figure 3.7 Collar brace joints.

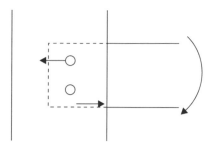

Figure 3.8 Forces on a pegged mortice and tenon resisting a moment at the joint. This assumes no force on one of the pegs although in practice there may be forces on both.

the shoulder of the tenon and the sides of the mortice. A corresponding tension force must be generated if the joint is to resist the applied moment, and this will be in the further peg. This is how the joints in a close studded wall without braces would be acting if we assume that the infill provides no racking resistance. In such a wall any racking forces will be distributed across a large number of joints, producing correspondingly low forces in each. But the same effect might be seen in the timbers of a heavy frame.[*]

Some experimental work has been carried out on the racking resistance of framing in the context of modern heavy timber frames in North America (Brungraber, 1985). Unfortunately such results cannot be applied to historic structures because we are dealing with buildings where we know little about the initial standards of carpentry nor the extent to which any original moment carrying capacity may have been reduced by the effects of wetting and decay. The uncertain degree of 'prestress' produced by the process of assembly makes it difficult to assess the behaviour of joints and in particular the moments that they might be able to carry. It may therefore be safer to assume that joints are pinned and that we are dealing with a braced, pin-jointed frame with the braces allowed to take compression only. This is the approach adopted for the analysis of the frames.

---

[*] Little work has been done on the contribution of infill to the racking resistance of timber frames. Brick noggin must offer considerable resistance compared with that of the frame itself, but the important question is the contribution to racking resistance provided by traditional wattle and daub infill. Some work has been done in Japan in relation to this, where traditional infilling of timber frames with woven bamboo and clay infill is an important contribution to the earthquake resistance of traditional buildings.

The lap dovetail

Outward thrust of the rafters on wall plates is resisted by tension in the tie beams (Figure 3.9) and for this to be possible there has to be an appropriate connection between the wall plate and the tie beam. This is handled by connecting the two with a lap dovetail joint in which the load is transmitted across the shoulders of the joint (Figure 3.10). The forces on the side of the joint are oblique to the direction of the force and it is their component perpendicular to the wall plate that is

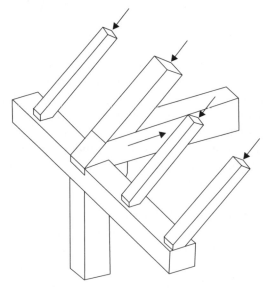

Figure 3.9 *Outward thrust on wall plate resisted by tie beam.*

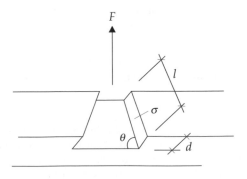

$$2\sigma dl \cos\theta = F$$

Figure 3.10 *Lap dovetail.*

resisting the force. Given the angle of the dovetail, rather high compressive stresses can be produced (see Chapter 5). However, the situation is more complex than this. Shrinkage of the tie beam will result in the dovetail becoming loose in its housing, so there is a tendency for the wall plate to move outward to keep the joint tight. Moreover, shrinkage of both the wall plate and the tie beam will change the geometry of the joint so that the timbers may be bearing over a much smaller area than that assumed in the diagram. It is of course the face of the male part of the joint that is critical, where the load is more or less perpendicular to the grain. Any enhancement of the allowable stress by applying Hankinson's formula will be modest. Thus the compressive stress on the sides of the joint can be compared with an allowable compressive stress of 4 N/mm^2 for oak loaded perpendicular to the grain (assuming no wane). In some structures the lap dovetail is made more complex to provide a greater angle (Figure 3.11), and this is obviously more effective because the compressive stresses will be smaller and the geometry of the joint is less affected by shrinkage.

This brings us to the most complex joint in English carpentry, that between the tie beam wall plate and supporting post (Figure 3.12). The post is tenoned both into the wall plate and into the tie beam. The tendency for outward movement of the wall plate as the lap dovetail shrinks is resisted by the two tenons, which have a fixed distance

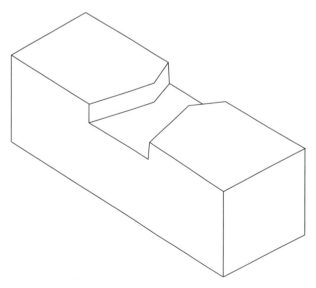

Figure 3.11 A lap dovetail cut to increase the angle of the active part of the joint. This has the effect of reducing the stresses on the mating faces.

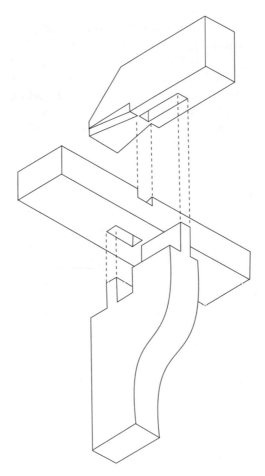

Figure 3.12 Post/wall plate/tie beam joint.

between them. This induces tensile forces at the top of the post across the grain that will be exacerbated by shrinkage across the grain of timber. The result is that these posts commonly show splitting of these post jowls. Dramatic though this 'failure' may appear it has little structural significance.

Scarf joints

In medieval structures, scarf joints were used between continuous lengths of plates and purlins, the joints generally positioned close to where the member was supported by a frame. Cecil Hewett (1980:

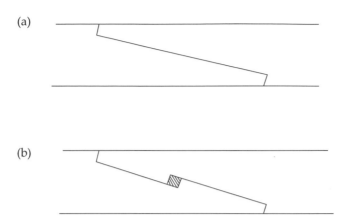

(a)

(b)

Figure 3.13 Simple forms of scarf joint.

263–71) has produced a large catalogue of scarf joints, ostensibly in chronological order, but we need only deal with a relatively small number here. Some of these may need to be repaired or replaced in conservation work. In other circumstances new scarf joints are made to join new timber to the original material where there has been decay of the latter, although these are commonly made with modern fasteners rather than with pegs (see Chapter 7). The simple tabled scarf with undersquinted abutments (Figure 3.13(a)) is ideal for joining lengths of purlins. With the member loaded perpendicular to the plane of the joint and with the joint close to or over the supporting frame there would only be a shear force to be transmitted. Where it is used in modern repair work the joint is often called upon to carry bending moments. Where a joint is used to connect lengths of tie beams in later roofs the variation with a central key to transmit tension forces (Figure 3.13(b)) is better, the key also allowing the shoulders of the abutments to be drawn tight.

The tabled scarf joint is far from ideal if loaded in the other plane, because then the pegs would have to carry the shear force. Therefore the bridle scarf was commonly used in wall plates in order to transmit the horizontal thrust of the rafters (Figure 3.14). A weakness of this joint is that it was commonly made off centre, which reduces the section available to carry load, and failure of these joints has sometimes been seen. This occurs by splitting along the grain from the root of the mortice. What might also not have been apparent is that as the rafters bear against the top outer edge of the plate they impose torsion force on the joint as well as the direct forces, and this too must be transmitted across the joint.

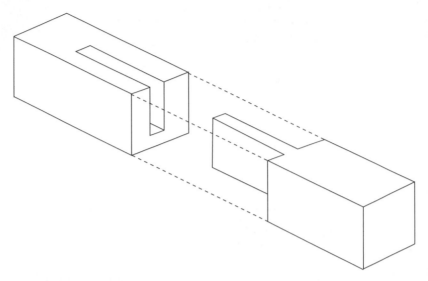

Figure 3.14 A wall plate bridle scarf.

Joints for softwood structures

The distinguishing feature of the new carpentry was the need to carry
tension forces. Any load on the tie beam of a truss had to be carried in
tension by the king post, or in later trusses by the queen posts. It was
also important to ensure that the outward thrusts of the principal rafters were adequately restrained by the tie beam. The purely carpentry
device for fastening the king post to the tie beam relied upon a wedged
half dovetail (Figure 3.15) that could be assembled and then tightened
by driving in the wedge. This does not seem to have been commonly
used and had the disadvantage that it required undercutting the tenon.
Instead, carpenters turned to the blacksmith to provide them with
metal straps and bolts: initially forelock bolts, but eventually coach
bolts (Figure 3.16). Using this device the bolts had to transfer load
between a relatively thin metal strap and a large timber section,
although these were often used in conjunction with pegged mortice
and tenon joints, so that it is not always clear exactly how the load is
being transmitted. Of course, shrinkage of timbers might well result in
straps becoming loose. Trusses have been seen in which a wedge was
driven between the strap and the soffit of the tie – but these too are
often loose. In long-span trusses where the tie beam is formed in two
halves and cannot take bending, support provided by the king-post
strap is critical.

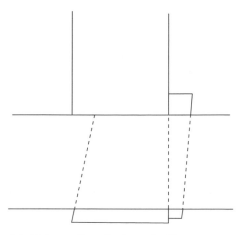

Figure 3.15 Wedged half dovetail at the foot of a king post.

In the 19th century more positive fastenings came into use for connecting king or queen posts to the tie beam. The metal strap could be fixed with cotters and folding wedges (Figure 3.16(a)), suitable for large trusses, but the most commonly seen device is a bolt through the tie beam and up into the foot of the post. This was held in the post by a caged nut within the timber, often covered by a small plug (Figure 3.16(b)). Both devices allow the tie beam to be tightened up against the bottom of the posts so that there is no movement before load is taken

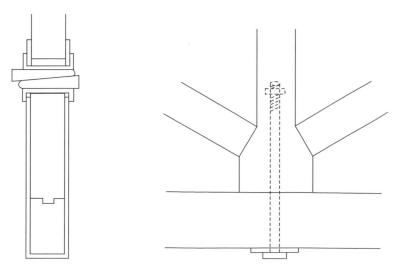

Figure 3.16 Nineteenth century fasteners for the bottom of the king post. (a) Cotters and folding wedges; (b) long bolt with caged nut.

up. In American bridge construction bolts provided the potential to be tightened up if there was any shrinkage of the timbers (Nelson, 1996) but there is no evidence that they were used in this way in Britain.

The most crucial joint in the softwood truss is the heel joint where the principal rafters thrust against the ends of the tie beam. Roger Pratt's recommendation that the feet of the principals 'be very strongly footed, bolted and keyed to prevent the kicking of them up' gives the impression that the metalwork there was simply a locating device while the carpentry was to carry the thrusts from the principals into the tie beam. Whatever the intention of these straps, they too are often loose. However, the stitch bolt through the heel joint of trusses had a much greater chance of carrying load if necessary, although one would anticipate some slippage of the joint in doing so.

An important 19th century development was the introduction of bridle joints, which came to replace mortice and tenon joints in the heel joints of roof trusses. These were recommended in textbooks because the bearing surfaces of the joint are visible and the workmanship could be checked. In this joint the thrust of the principal rafter comes directly onto the tie beam at the bearing surfaces rather than the horizontal and vertical components of the force being taken separately (Figure 3.17).

Another 19th century development was to use doubled posts clasped round the tie beam and principal rafter. The posts were notched where the other members intersected them and were held together with bolts (Figure 3.18). In some cases the bolts are there simply to hold the two parts of the post together, in which case forces must be transferred

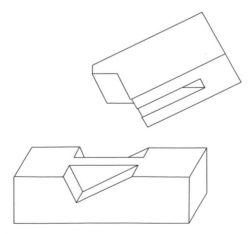

Figure 3.17 Bridle joint to form the heel joint of a roof truss.

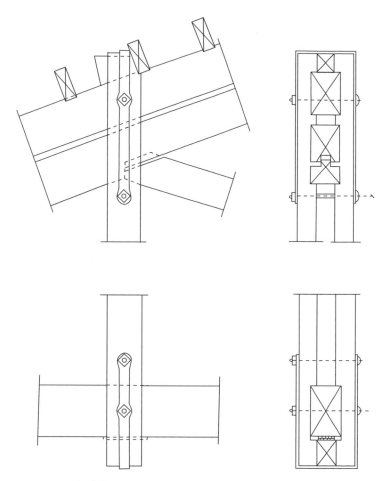

Figure 3.18 Detail of the construction of a truss with double posts.

directly between the timber surfaces. In other cases, bolts may pass through the intersecting timbers, either the tie beam or principal rafters, and then there must be some question about the extent to which the forces at the joint are transferred between the timbers or through the bolt.

Iron castings were screwed or bolted to timbers either as a means of transferring load between two timbers or to connect iron tie rods. In framing large warehouses spreaders were commonly used at the tops of columns to carry beam loads. Initially these were of timber, but this was clearly unsatisfactory. While compression stresses at the ends of the beams would be reduced, those on the spreader itself where it bore on the column would still be high compared with the capacity of the timber, and crushing of spreaders can be seen in some buildings. Of course, this would not lead to a collapse as the timber has nowhere to go, but it must result in some settlement of the frame compared with the enclosing masonry walls. Long cast-iron column caps were the solution to this problem and these remained in use, with cast iron columns and timber beams a not uncommon combination.

4

Behaviour of oak frames

Distribution of the loads in any kind of timber framing will depend not only upon the original framing arrangement but also upon changes that have occurred since the original construction. Of course many of these will have been deliberate changes as the building was adapted from time to time to more modern uses. Therefore each will be unique to the particular building, although there are some common alterations, such as the replacement of wattle and daub infill with brickwork and the insertion of upper floors into what were once open halls. There are also some parts of the construction that are more vulnerable to decay and insect attack than others, so that there are some commonly found weaknesses in frames that have led to redistribution of the loads. However, even if there have been no deliberate changes to the structure and there is minimal decay, the method of framing and the behaviour of the material will have resulted in some redistribution of loads, largely as a result of shrinkage of the timbers and creep deflections.

The timber was worked green, so there will have been some subsequent drying shrinkage. Oak shrinks by about 5% of its original dimension across the grain, which is significant. The way in which this affects load transmission in the frame needs to be discussed, but first we need to consider the effect on the overall movement of frames. In a basic box frame construction with jettied floors there is a considerable thickness of cross-grain timber that is transmitting load. The wall plate rests on the studs, which in turn are carried by the bressummer or jetty sill. This is carried by the joists, which in turn rest on the head plate of the wall frame below. Thus, assuming a two-storey building, between the top of the ground floor plate and the underside of the wall plate there will be two plate thicknesses and the thickness of the joists. This can amount to as much as 25 in (635 mm) (or more), which would have a shrinkage of over 1.25 in (32 mm). At the rear of the building the main frames have posts that are continuous over both storeys so that there will be no such shrinkage. The effect of such differential shrinkage between the front and rear walls is for the building to lean forward slightly, and in a three-storey building the effect will be that much greater.

The other effect is creep, mainly affecting purlin roofs, because it is the roof purlins that are likely to carry the greatest bending load while still green. Booth and Reece (1967: 68), in their commentary on CP112, cite research that indicates an average creep deflection under these conditions of 3.5 times the elastic deflection, but with an extreme value of 7 times the elastic deflection.

Both of these effects, shrinkage and creep, will result in changes in the load path within the frames as members originally carrying load have shed all or part of that load to other members. Therefore, before considering the actual loads and stresses in the structure, it is useful to begin with a qualitative description of its behaviour.

These buildings were constructed as framed structures and some of them do act in this way. However, examination of box-framed buildings shows that while they have all the appearance of frames they work largely as load-bearing wall structures and it is only in resisting wind loads that we find any frame action. This means that in considering the vertical and horizontal loading we are looking at quite different structures. Moreover, as already noted, it is prudent to assume that braces in the frames only act in compression, with the effect that horizontal loads acting in each direction are resisted by rather different structures. There is only space here to consider a few of possible framing arrangements, but making a qualitative description of its structural behaviour is a sensible first step in the analysis of any building. Because the distribution of forces is affected by shrinkage of the timbers, by creep deflections and by decay of some of the members, the overall effects of these cannot be accurately predicted, so that it is often useful to consider alternative load paths.

Loads

The vertical loads on a timber frame are principally the weight of the roof covering, the loads on the floor and the self-weight of the structure flooring and wall infill. All of these are subject to change, although changes to the timber structure will not affect its self-weight significantly. Perhaps the most common change in the roofing has been the replacement of thatch roofs with more durable materials. Where the latter are stone slates the effect can be particularly severe, possibly increasing the stresses in roof purlins to values close to, or even above, those allowed by modern design codes. The weight of walls will be increased when wattle and daub infill is replaced with brick nogging. In the past the live loads on floors would have been comparatively low, and certainly nothing like those demanded by modern design codes. This is especially true when timber frame buildings are to be used for other than domestic purposes; for example, restaurants or offices, for which higher design loads are required. However, the sizes of floor members are normally such that stresses are within acceptable limits providing that good quality timbers were used in the construction.

The roof is subject to snow loads, but these can be small compared with the self-weight of the covering. As timber is able to carry higher loads for short periods of time than the permanent loads that it can sustain it is the percentage increase that such temporary loads produce that is significant. Often for historic buildings these will be found to be within the increase in stress allowed for medium-term loads. Snow load is simply an additional vertical load, while wind loads have to be carried by different structural actions. Wind loading will produce bending stresses in wall studs, but these will be sufficiently low that they can be ignored. Also, any increase in bending in rafters or purlins as a result of positive wind pressures on the roof will often be within the allowable increase in stress for short-term loads. For timber-framed buildings friction forces between the frame and the masonry plinth will be sufficient to resist overall wind forces, so that the principal concern will be the provision of adequate bracing in the structure to ensure its stability. The forces in braces will not be insignificant because horizontal timbers – the purlins and plates – will serve to transmit the wind loads from large areas of roof and wall to the transverse frames.

The wind loads on a building depend upon the basic wind speed, the degree of exposure and the size of the building. The basic wind speed depends upon the location of the building, and the code of practice provides a map of wind speeds across the country. This is modified to obtain a design wind speed that depends upon the degree of exposure; a building on an exposed hill with no wind breaks will naturally be subject to larger wind loads than a building in the middle of a nearby town. Also a tall building will be subjected to higher wind speeds because ground friction slows the wind. From the design wind speed the wind pressures are determined from pressure coefficients that will be different for each building surface. As wind passes round the building negative pressures will be created on the leeward face and the

A simple calculation for the wind load at right angles to the axis of the building shows the magnitude of wind loads that can occur. Assume the roof is covered by plain clay tiles on a 45° slope. BS 648 gives the weight of tiles as 71 kg/m² resulting in 980 N/m² measured on plan. If the building is divided into bays by frames at 4 m centres the load/frame can be calculated to be approximately 23.4 kN.

In an area where the basic wind speed is 44 m/s, i.e. most of the midlands of England, and in open country with scattered wind breaks, the design wind pressure may be estimated from CP3 Chapter 5 and the wind loads obtained.

Pressure coefficients on the walls and roof are as shown in Figure 4.1. Only half of the wind load on the walls has to be resisted by the frames, the remainder being taken by wall studs to the ground. Using these coefficients the horizontal load to be resisted by each frame is approximately 8.6 kN.

From the results it is clear that the wind is not an insignificant load. It is about a third of the vertical load for this building. A steeper roof pitch would produce a more dramatic wind effect and wind would become a larger proportion of the self-weight if either pantiles @ 40 kg/m² or Welsh slates @ 25 kg/m² were used.

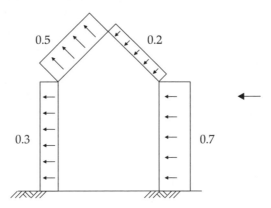

Figure 4.1 Wind loads on a frame.

side walls. Internal pressures are important when calculating the forces on elements of cladding, and this could be a serious issue in buildings such as barns that could have large openings. However, internal pressures have a neutral effect on the overall wind loads to be resisted by the structure. Moreover, for a simple rectangular building the positive and negative pressures on the windward and leeward surfaces can simply be added together to determine the forces to be resisted by the braces.

Rafter forces

Coupled rafter roof

The forces on a coupled rafter roof are the simplest place to begin. If two rafters lean against each other to support the covering this means that at the apex each rafter produces a horizontal force to support the other. Because the forces on any structural member must be in balance there must be an equal and opposite horizontal force provided by whatever is supporting the rafter, i.e. the wall plate, as well as the vertical force that is equal to the downward force on the rafter. This is normally described the other way round; we say that the rafters impose a vertical load on the wall plate and also thrust outward (Figure 4.2(a)). To resist this outward thrust the wall plates must be tied together with tie beams at intervals along the length of the building. Between these ties the wall plate will be in bending as a result of the horizontal thrust.

The magnitude of the horizontal forces can be found in several ways, but the simplest is to take moments about the foot of the rafter. If the span of the rafter from wall plate to apex = 1, and the height of the roof = h, then $Wl/2 = Hh$.

In practice it is more convenient to work with the span and length of the rafters because the latter can be measured more easily than the height of the roof. Thus in the above formula the substitutions $l = a \cos \theta$ and $h = a \sin \theta$ can be made.

For a 45° pitch $l = h$, from which we can see that $H = W/2$, and as the roof pitch is reduced the horizontal force will increase.

Collar-braced rafters

The rafters themselves will tend to deflect under the load of the covering material, and to prevent this common rafter roofs are normally braced with collars between each pair of rafters. While the intention is to reduce the bending in the rafters, a simple consideration of the forces (Figure 4.3) will show that this advantage is gained at the expense of some increase in the outward thrust on the wall plate. Of course the force in the collar will depend upon its position on the rafter. In some

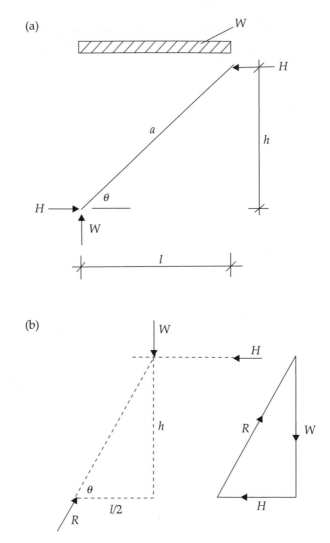

Figure 4.2 Free body diagram for a coupled rafter.

cases collars are at the mid-point of the rafter, but it was normal to have
them at about 2/3 of the height. The former is the more efficient in terms
of reducing the moments in the rafter. The effect of raising the collar is
to reduce the force within it, as well as reducing the length of the collar,
which in turn reduces the outward thrust on the wall plate. Because the
collar is in compression there would be some tendency for it to buckle
under load, and reducing both the length and the compressive force

There are two other ways of obtaining the horizontal forces. They may be obtained graphically by drawing a triangle of forces for the forces on the rafter (Figure 4.2(b)). For this the horizontal and vertical forces at the rafter foot are combined into the single reaction R. There are then three forces that must meet at a point that can then be redrawn as a triangle of forces. The geometry of this triangle is such that $W/H = h/(l/2)$.

Alternatively, one may resolve the forces at the foot of the rafter. This is more complex because there is both a shear force and a direct force in the rafter. The shear force $= (W/2)\cos\theta$. If the compressive stress at the rafter foot $= C$, then considering vertical equilibrium at the rafter foot:

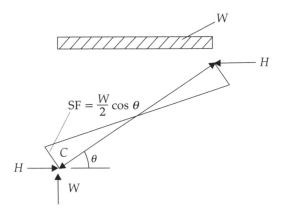

$W = C\sin\theta + (W/2)\cos^2\theta$, i.e. $C = (W - (W/2)\cos^2\theta)/\sin\theta$

For horizontal equilibrium:

$$H = C\cos\theta - (W/2)\cos\theta\sin\theta$$
$$= (W - (W/2)\cos^2\theta)\cos\theta/\sin\theta - (W/2)\cos\theta\sin\theta$$
$$= (W - W/2(1 - \sin^2\theta))\cos\theta/\sin\theta - (W/2)\cos\theta\sin^2\theta/\sin\theta$$
$$= W\cos\theta/\sin\theta - (W/2)\cos\theta/\sin\theta$$
$$= (W/2)\cos\theta/\sin\theta$$

would help to avoid this. However, it is only rarely that compressive stresses will be sufficiently high for buckling to be a concern.

The force in the collar can be found by considering the bending of the rafters. Each is a continuous beam carried on three supports each of which can be considered to be rigid (i.e. they do not deflect under load). By determining the bending moments in this beam under a uniformly distributed load the support reactions can be found.

The simplest way to do this is by moment distribution. For readers who are familiar with this, the fixed end moments for each span are those of a propped cantilever and the moment at the intermediate support is then obtained from a single distribution. This allows the moment and forces to be found for any position of the collar, but in practice there are two common positions for the collar, either halfway up the rafters or two thirds of the way up.

The figures in Figure 4.4, as well as in Table 4.1 (p. 76), are expressed as ratios of the total load. Thus the actual forces can be obtained by multiplying these by the total load on the rafter.

Note that with the collar at 1/3 height the sagging moment in the lower part of the rafter will be found to be greater than the hogging moment at the collar. With the collar at the mid-point the sagging and hogging moments on the rafter are equal.

Referring to Figure 4.4, the support reactions for a two-span beam with the collar both at mid-point and two thirds up the rafter are shown. With the collar force known the collar-braced roof can be treated in a similar way to the coupled rafter roof, i.e. considering only one half with an external horizontal force at the apex; the support force provided by the other rafter. This horizontal force at the apex comprises an axial force in the rafter and a shear force, the latter being the support force required by the two-span beam (Figure 4.5). Given this known force and the slope of the roof, the horizontal force can be found. The

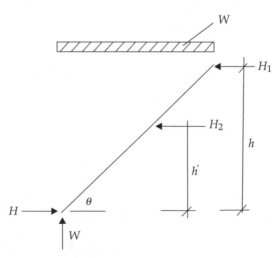

Figure 4.3 Free body diagram for a collar braced rafter

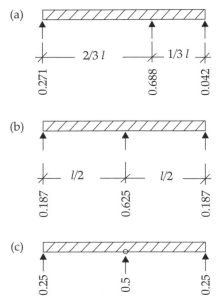

Figure 4.4 Two span beams showing support reactions for different positions of the supports: (a) at the third point; (b) at mid-point; c) at mid-point with two simply supported spans.

force in the collar must be such that its component perpendicular to the rafter is the required support reaction at the centre of the two-span beam. (The third force in the triangle of forces is the change in the axial force in the rafter at this point.) The two horizontal forces can now be added to give the horizontal force at the wall plate. The effect of collars at different pitches can be seen from Table 4.1. The figures represent the forces as a ratio of the load on a rafter. From this it is clear that having the collars at the mid-point of the rafters has a greater effect on wall plate load.

Table 4.1 assumes that there is no spreading at the feet of the rafters. In timber-framed buildings outward deflection of the wall plate will have the effect of reducing the outward thrust causing that deflection, so affecting the bending moments in the rafters.

Purlin roof

The alternative to bracing is for the rafters to be assisted by purlins that in turn are supported by some kind of frame. The purlin will be a halved timber and the effect of the method of conversion is that the

Pitch $\theta°$	40	45	50	55	60
Unbraced rafter – H =	0.6	0.50	0.42	0.35	0.29
Collar at mid point					
Apex force – H_1 =	0.22	0.19	0.16	0.13	0.11
Collar force – H_2 =	0.74	0.63	0.52	0.44	0.36
Wall plate force – H =	0.97	0.81	0.68	0.57	0.47
Collar at 2/3 rafter height					
Apex force – H_1 =	0.15	0.13	0.10	0.09	0.07
Collar force – H_2 =	0.57	0.48	0.40	0.34	0.28
Wall plate force – H =	0.72	0.60	0.51	0.42	0.35

Table 4.1 Horizontal forces on unbraced and collar-braced rafters.

sawn surface is the only guaranteed straight line in the timber. For this reason that would be the surface placed under the rafters. This is the larger cross-sectional dimension. The result is that the smaller cross-sectional dimension is perpendicular to the slope, so that the deflection of the purlins under rafter load will also be perpendicular to the slope. Therefore the support reaction that they provide will be at right angles to the rafters rather than the horizontal force provided by the collar. The upward component of this force has the effect of relieving the wall plate of some of the rafter load, but the extent to which purlins are able to do this depends upon the extent to which they deflect. Any deflection of the purlins means that they provide less support to the rafters, so increasing the load on the wall plate. Moreover, purlin deflection is

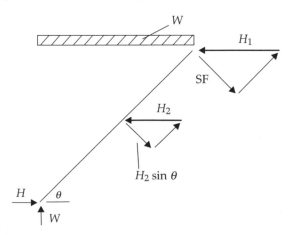

Figure 4.5 Free body diagram for a collar braced rafter with the components perpendicular and parallel to the rafter of the apex and collar forces.

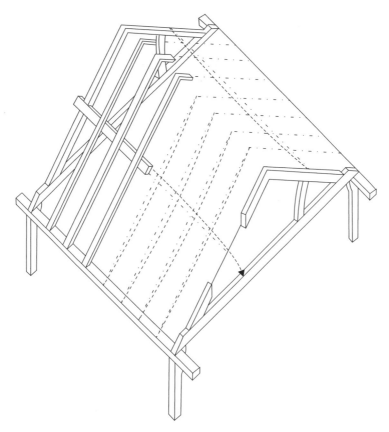

Figure 4.6 Deflections in a purlin roof.

not simply a matter of initial elastic deflection as the load is applied. Because the purlins are loaded while the timber is still green there will be considerable creep deflection. This explains the commonly seen distortion of early roofs, where the position of the frames can be clearly seen from the shape of the roof (Figure 4.6). Sometimes of course there are large deflections because the original roof covering has been replaced with a much heavier material.

With reliable data on the properties of both rafters and purlin it would be possible to do a full elastic analysis of their behaviour, but in reality it is very difficult to assign sensible figures to these properties. It would also be a useless exercise because creep deflection has a far more significant effect on long-term deflections. Therefore the simplest way to examine the behaviour of the roof is to consider two limiting conditions: one in which the purlins are assumed to be straight and rigid, and one in which the purlins have deflected to such an extent that the

Given the assumptions discussed, the reaction $R = 1.25\ (W/2)\cos\theta$, while the shear force at each end of the rafter $= 0.375\ (W/2)\cos\theta$.

The forces at the apex are the shear force and axial force in the rafter and a horizontal force provided by the other rafter. Thus the value of the horizontal force may be obtained by drawing a triangle of forces for these three forces (Figure 4.7).

$$H'\sin\theta = 0.375(W/2)\cos\theta$$
$$H = H' + R\sin\theta = 0.375(W/2)\cos\theta/\sin\theta + 1.25(W/2)\cos\theta\sin\theta$$

Considering vertical equilibrium,

$$V = W - 1.25(W/2)\cos^2\theta$$

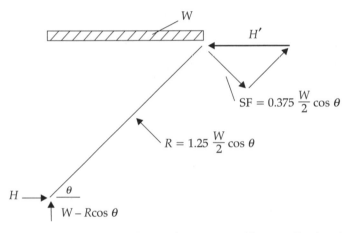

Figure 4.7 *Free body diagram for a rafter supported by a purlin showing the components of the force at the apex perpendicular and parallel to the rafter.*

rafters are unassisted. The former gives a value for the load on the purlin that is unlikely to be achieved in practice, because they must deflect to some extent.

The purlin is normally half way up the slope of the roof so that each rafter can be treated as a two-span beam over a rigid support as before to determine the support reaction from the purlin (Figure 4.4(b)). At the apex of the roof there is a shear force and an axial force in the rafter, which, since the arrangement is symmetrical, result in a horizontal force on the opposite rafter. Knowing the direction and magnitude of the shear force and the direction of the other two forces means that a triangle of forces can be drawn at the apex of the roof, giving the magnitude of the horizontal support force. The horizontal force at the wall plate is then the sum of this horizontal force and the horizontal component of the support reaction provided by the purlin.

To obtain some idea of the effect of the purlins these values can be compared with those for free spanning rafters for three different roof slopes.

Values for H at	60°	45°	30°
With purlin	0.38W	0.5W	0.59W
Without purlin	0.29W	0.5W	0.87W

From this it can be seen that for a 45° slope the outward force exerted by the rafters at their feet is the same for both conditions (although this could have been demonstrated algebraically). In other words, the deflection of the purlins under load has no effect on the horizontal forces on the wall plate. Most of the roofs of this period are at about 45°

Occasionally a roof will have two pairs of purlins, but this can be solved in a similar way. Figure 4.8 shows the support reactions for such a roof with the triangle of forces at the apex. Based on this, $H' \sin\theta = (0.4W \cos\theta)/3$, i.e. $H' = (0.4W \cos\theta/3)\sin\theta$.

$$H = 2(1.1W \cos\theta \sin\theta)/3 + (0.4W \cos\theta)/3\sin\theta$$
$$= W \cos\theta(2.2\sin\theta + 0.4\sin\theta)/3$$

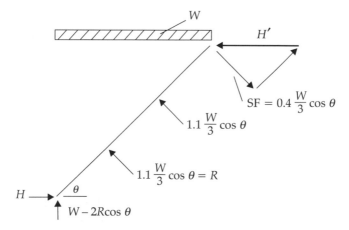

Figure 4.8 Free body diagram for a rafter supported by a pair of purlins at the third points.

slope – in fact very slightly greater than this, but to an extent that can be ignored for this purpose. Thus we can check the outward thrust of the roofs and hence the likely bending stress on the wall plate with some confidence, simply by ignoring the purlin. For many purposes it may be adequate to assume that $H = W/2$.

This discussion assumes that the rafters are not pegged to the purlins. Where they are, any outward movement of the wall plate will result in some load being applied to the purlin in the plane of the roof. The result will be a reduction in loads on the wall plate.

As well as the forces on the wall plate, the effect of purlin deflection on bending in the rafters also needs to be considered. Consider first a beam carrying a load W over a span l; then the bending moment is $Wl/8$. If the same beam is supported at mid-span then the maximum moment in hogging over the support is given as $W'l'/8$, where W' is the load on each of the spans and l' the length of each span. Of course $W' = W/2$ and $l' = l/2$, so that this moment is a quarter of the moment on an unassisted rafter. Put the other way round, deflection of the purlin can result in a fourfold increase in the moment on the rafter, and from hogging to sagging. It will also be apparent that the hogging moment on a continuous two-span beam has the same numerical value as the sagging moment on two simply supported beams (Figure 4.4(c)). In other words, a continuous rafter could be replaced by two short rafters with no increase in the value of the moment. If the continuous rafters are adequate to carry the load but some have decayed, replacement of half spans of the same size would also be adequate in terms of strength although their stiffness would be less. Perhaps counter-intuitively this change also results in a reduction of the load on the purlin of 4/5.

Note that all of these calculations assume that there is no taper in the rafters, whereas there often is in practice. Clearly the extent of the error will depend upon the degree of taper, which is not significant in many cases.

Purlin support

In some roofs the purlins are carried on principal rafters that are strutted with a collar at or near the position of the purlin. In such cases the forces in the principal rafter can be found by assuming that the joint between collar and principals is tightly made, in which case the timber above the collar can be ignored and the frame treated as a simple arch of three members. Where the principal is strutted from the tie beam, load

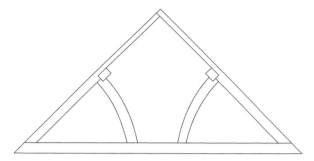

Figure 4.9 A simple form of roof frame in which the purlins are strutted from the tie beam.

must either be transmitted to the tie, where it is carried in bending, be carried by the principal rafter in bending if the struts are ineffective or shared between the two. The actual load-carrying mechanism will depend upon the structural layout, the relative sizes of the members, the quality of the original carpentry and the degree of shrinkage that has occurred since its construction. With the heavy tie beams and relatively small principals of some early roofs the struts might be expected to transmit purlin loads to the tie, but shrinkage of both principals and tie beam might well result in a relaxation of the force in the struts, with the principals required to carry some of the purlin load.

Some roofs have relatively light principals set above the purlins, which are simply strutted from the tie beam (Figure 4.9). Many later roofs of this kind have relatively light tie beams, and this is often an unsatisfactory design. Purlin loads are being carried by the longest timber in the roof, the tie beam, and this might be inadequate to resist the bending stresses thus imposed. This kind of roof often requires some strengthening.

The effect of shrinkage in members of the roof frame can be clearly seen in clasped purlin roofs, where the purlins are supported on a collar strutted from the tie beam rather than by the principal rafters (Figure 2.8(a)). The sequence of assembly suggests the mechanism of load transfer. The posts would have been stood on the tie beam and the collar then placed on these. The purlins would then be put in position and finally the principal rafters. Thus it seems obvious that the loads on the purlins are transmitted by the posts to the relatively stiff tie beam (Figure 4.10(a)). However, we often see buildings in which there is a gap between the bottom of these posts and the tie beam – presumably the result of shrinkage in the tie. In such circumstances there can be no load in the posts, so that the purlin loads must be being transmitted from the

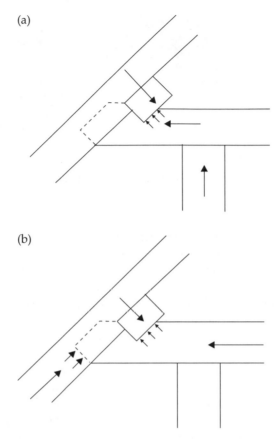

(a)

(b)

Figure 4.10   Alternative force diagrams for a clasped purlin roof.

collar to the principal rafters (Figure 4.10(b)). This means that the stresses in the principal/collar joint may need to be considered, and it also means that there will be a direct force in the principal rafter to be resisted by the mortice in the tie beam that receives the rafter.

Wind loading on the roof

Wind loading on the side of the roof produces a positive pressure on the windward side and a negative pressure on the leeward side. The effect of this on common rafter roofs is to introduce bending in the rafters. In the tall, steep-pitched roofs of cathedrals wind loading produces con-siderably larger bending stresses in the rafters than does the dead load,

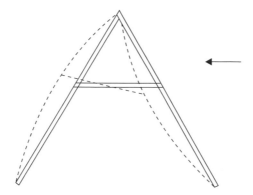

Figure 4.11 Deflection of a collar braced roof under wind loading.

although the wind-load stress will of course be temporary. The collar constrains the two rafters to move equally (Figure 4.11) and it is in resisting these wind loads that bracing between rafters and collar comes into effect. In some cases these braces are extended to form scissor braces. The behaviour of this kind of roof has been discussed by Heyman (1976) in relation to the roof of Westminster Abbey.

In crown-post roofs longitudinal horizontal forces are gathered by the collar plate and transmitted to the crown post and its bracing. This will result in some bending on the crown post and the collar plate. The horizontal force on the crown post will in turn be resisted by bending in the tie beam, but all these forces will be small and racking of these roofs is not usually a problem. Purlin roofs are commonly constructed with braces between the purlins and each pair of principal rafters to stabilise the roof, and it is these that carry the wind forces on the gable. With a large number of braces to carry the comparatively low wind load on the gable end, provision for this is more than adequate. Both the force in the braces and the consequent bending stresses in the purlins will be low. Of course, if a number of braces are broken the load on the remaining braces will be correspondingly higher and the stresses may need to be checked.

The box frame

Cruck frames were dealt with first in the Chapter 2, but although their construction is simpler than box frames they present a little more difficulty in analysis. Therefore in this chapter box frames are dealt with

(a) (b)

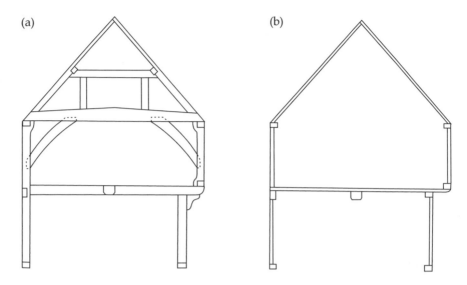

Figure 4.12 Sections through a jettied timber-frame building. The section that does not show the frame makes clear the construction as a load-bearing wall structure.

first. Although the buildings comprise a series of transverse frames (Figure 4.12(a)) these might only carry a small proportion of the roof load. If we consider a typical section rather than the section at the frame we can see that the studs below the wall plate bear onto the plates at first floor level (Figure 4.12(b)). It is unlikely that the wall plate would be stiffer than the wall, even allowing for the deflection of the jettied (i.e. cantilevered) floor joists at the front. Therefore the only part of the roof load to be carried back to the main frames will be that picked up by the purlins, the remainder being carried by the wall studs. At the front, the load will be delivered to the jettied floor joists. Given the tendency of the purlins to creep under load, this 'remainder' could be a large proportion of the roof load. The effect of this on the cantilevered joists at the front of the building is that they may well be in hogging over their whole length when the floor is carrying no live load. The ground floor walls will support the plates at first floor level. It is clear from this that wall plates only have to carry significant vertical roof loads in bending when they are spanning over openings such as waggon-ways that gave access to the rear of the building or over the front of Wealden houses.

In Wealden houses, in which the wings either side of the hall are jettied, a substantial load from the central wall plate at the front will have to be transmitted to the cross frames via the braces because the plate itself will be inadequate. (The same is true of the arcade plates of aisled structures.) The plate should therefore be treated as a three-span beam. In making repairs the carpenter might wish to ensure that these braces carry their full load by tightening the mortice and tenon joints by driving wedges into the end of the mortice.

Floor structures have a simple layout, with joists framed into a central beam that in turn is carried by the transverse members of the cross frames. The issue of shear forces in the tenons has already been discussed. Note that in calculating the shear stress in a rectangular section it is the maximum stress that has to be calculated, not the average stress. For a simple rectangular section this means that the maximum shear stress, which occurs at the neutral axis, i.e. the centre of the beam, is given by $1.5 \times$ shear force/area of cross-section.

Wind loads on the frame

An important function of the frames in all structures is to resist the wind loads. The simplest way to understand the bracing of a frame is first to consider a simple rectangular frame with a horizontal force. This is the kind of structure that one would find in a very simple barn (Figure 4.13). This wind force will tend to overturn the structure. Forces at the sole plates can be found simply by taking moments about the foot of one of the plates. The weight of the structure must be such that v_2 acts upwards, because if the weight is insufficient some hold-down force will be required. Ignoring the roof and assuming that the wind simply results in a horizontal force at the wall plate, if braces can only act in compression we have the structure shown in Figure 4.14(a). Only the brace on the leeward side of the building is acting to carry the wind load. With the other post effectively hinged at both ends, all wind load

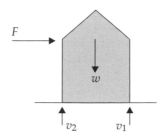

Figure 4.13 Wind load and support forces on a simple structure to consider overall stability.

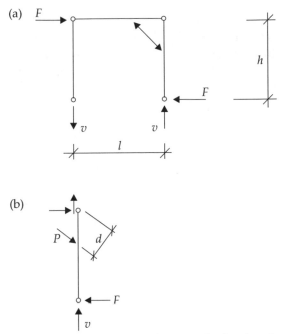

Figure 4.14 (a) A simple braced frame showing the bracing force that resists racking. (b) The free body diagram for the leeward leg of the frame showing the forces acting.

on the structure must be resisted by the ground at the base of this braced post, as shown.

To find the bracing forces a free body diagram is drawn for the braced post (Figure 4.14(b)). There are five forces on this: the horizontal and vertical forces at the ground, the force in the brace and forces at the top of the post from the beam. The beam clearly must transmit the horizontal wind force to the top of the post, but is also in bending because of the brace acting on it and so will have a shear force at the end. To find the force in the brace we may introduce the concept of 'bracing distance'. Without the brace rotation would take place about the inside of the joint. Resistance to this is provided by a force acting between the ends of the mortices within the beam and the post (see Figure 4.15). The bracing distance is measured from the point about which rotation would occur to the line joining these ends of the brace. Note therefore that the bracing distance is not the distance from the hinge to the brace itself, because if the brace is curved the bracing force will lie outside the brace. Although this means that the brace is in bending these members are normally broad enough for the stresses to be low. The bracing force

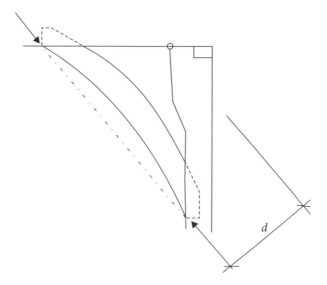

Figure 4.15 A corner brace showing the bracing distance d.

is simply found by considering moments about the top of the post where the unknown forces are acting.

In Figure 4.14(b) the bracing distance is given as d. Then, considering the forces on the braced post and taking moments about the top joint, $Fh = Pd$, where P is the force in the brace. Thus $P = Fh/d$.

Once the bracing force has been found the forces in the beam can also be found.

As braces are only assumed to be acting in compression and the jettied frame is asymmetric there are slightly different structures to consider for wind in different directions (Figure 4.16). If there are braces on both floors the resulting frames are statically indeterminate because the post at the rear of the building is continuous. The difficulty this presents is that it is not possible to tell how the bracing forces might be distributed between the two acting braces, partly because the relative stiffnesses of the members cannot be known precisely and partly because neither brace can be assumed to have perfectly tight joints. Of course, the frame can be reduced to a statically determinate structure by simply ignoring one or other of the active braces, and this gives us two possible structures to consider for each direction of wind; four in total. It is also possible to reduce the structure to one that is statically determinate by assuming the rear post to be discontinuous at the floor level. This produces two simple braced frames standing one on top of

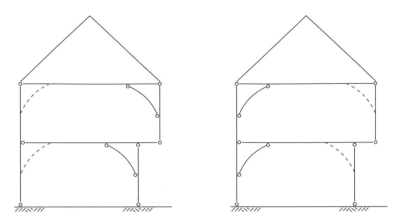

Figure 4.16 Alternative effective bracing arrangements depending on wind direction compared with the actual bracing arrangement.

the other. Thus there are six different conditions that can be considered, Figure 4.17 showing the three for one direction of wind, although it will quickly be apparent which of these produces the worst loading for each member and joint that needs to be examined.

Although these are all possible frames, the condition of the rear post often suggests that it would be prudent to consider both braces as acting, but with the post assumed to take no bending moment at the floor. This is because there are three mortices taken out of the post at this point, leaving little timber to resist any bending; decay or insect attack at this vulnerable section will weaken it still further.

As the braces go into compression they exert forces against the beams and posts into which they are framed. This will produce some bending moments on these members that need to be considered. It also requires restraining forces at their ends. These are not generally significant except for the downward force required at the end of the tie beam to resist the upward component of the force in the brace. Difficulty may be experienced if there are only very short braces on the upper floor, resulting in correspondingly high bracing forces. The author found for one building that with wind loads assessed according to the most recent code of practice the hold-down force required at the end of the tie beam was greater than could be supplied by the weight of the roof alone. If so, the joint between post and tie had to carry some tension force. Reverting to Code of Practice CP3 Chapter V gave lower forces that the roof could supply. As the frame had survived several hundred years of wind loading the reader is left to draw whichever of the alternative explanations he or she prefers.

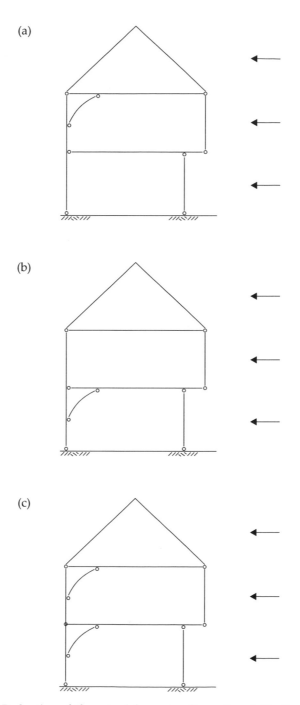

Figure 4.17 Reduction of the actual frame to alternative statically determinate frames.

Aisled frames

The scale of many aisled barn structures is much greater than the majority of domestic structures and there is no wall to support the arcade plate. The greater height of these buildings means that braces in the transverse frames will have to carry much greater wind forces, but it is also unlikely that an unassisted arcade plate would be able to carry the roof load without considerable deflection. Therefore the longitudinal braces will be assisting in carrying the roof load, and the arcade plate will have to be treated as a three-span beam, or more if it is continuous over two bays. However, there will be comparatively less horizontal bending on the arcade plate than an equivalent wall plate because of the aisle rafters. These are fastened to the outside face of the arcade plate from which they receive support in the form of a horizontal force, i.e. they simply lean against the arcade plate, producing an inward force that to some extent counteracts the outward thrust of the main rafters.

Outward thrust of the aisle rafters against the wall plate is resisted by aisle ties fastened to the main posts. Here the commonly used joint is a wedged half dovetail rather than a simple mortice and tenon joint. It is possible that this was adopted in recognition of the weakness of the mortice and tenon in direct tension. Although the joint relies upon shear parallel to the grain in the length of the tenon these joints have generally proved satisfactory. This dovetail has to take the whole of the outward thrust of the aisle rafters, but an assessment of the shear stress will show it to be low compared with that currently allowed by the code.

It is difficult to make any general comment on the bracing of aisled structures because of the wide variety of bracing arrangements that have been used. Even if the braces on the windward side of the building are eliminated, the remaining frame is still statically indeterminate and it is not possible to be sure how the bracing loads are distributed between the remaining active braces. This is not an academic issue because post feet might need replacing and the horizontal force at the foot of the post will depend upon how the wind load is shared between the main post and the corresponding wall post. It is also common to raise posts above the floor on masonry stylobates, and the stability of these might also be in question. The aisled barn of Figure 2.3 has passing braces that must make the aisle structure fairly stiff so that one might assume that the wind loads on each frame are shared between both the arcade post and the wall post. It is not possible to tell how the horizontal force is distributed between the two leeward posts, but as they are connected together by the lower plate across the aisle one might assume equal forces. Harmondsworth barn, the largest surviving aisled timber barn, has the aisle ties braced to both wall and arcade posts so that the framing on the windward side might also contribute to wind resistance.

In barns with much lighter aisle bracing it might be more prudent to assume that the leeward arcade post carries all forces to windward of it, with the wall post only taking the forces acting on the leeward aisle roof. Given the range of possible theoretical structures resisting the wind one first needs to examine the structure itself to see which of these models is reasonable. The engineer might then wish to carry out an elastic analysis of appropriate models, assuming pin joints, and to check the results against the actual structure to see whether the resulting forces are reasonable.

The cruck frame

Cruck frames are essentially arches and so impose horizontal thrusts on the supports although, given the height in relation to the span, the forces would be relatively small. The principal load on a cruck frame is the weight of the roof and the way in which this is carried depends upon the details of the frame. Ideally crucks should have sufficient curvature for the purlins to sit directly on them, but where this was not possible and where additional timbers were added to carry the purlins, these would impose a load on either an extended collar or on the cruck spurs (Figure 4.18). While the former is clearly able to carry the load in bending, the ability of the cruck spur to act as a cantilever depends upon the joint between it and the cruck blade. This is sometimes a notched lap joint and sometimes a mortice and tenon. Its cantilevering action would be compromised by any shrinkage of the cruck spur, allowing some rotation at the joint and resulting in the load on the cruck spur being picked up by the wall studs.

With the load from the purlins coming onto the cruck above the collar, the latter will be in compression as long as the feet of the blades are adequately restrained. However, outward movement of the feet will require the collar to be in tension and result in higher bending moments on the cruck blades. These are not uniform in cross-section, so the stresses may become critical in the narrower upper part of the blade. The possible effect of this can be seen by assuming no horizontal restraint at the foot of the cruck blade. The force at the apex will then be

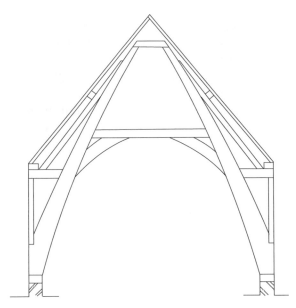

Figure 4.18 Diagram of a cruck frame with separate timbers to carry the purlins.

equal to tension force in the collar. This assumes that the pegs restraining the collar are capable of resisting this force. The horizontal force can be found by taking moments about this joint, when it becomes clear that the purlin load and the support reaction at the foot of the blade both produce a moment in the same direction. The maximum moment on the blade will occur under the purlin load, and cruck frames have been seen where movement of one or other of the blades because of insufficient restraint at the foot has resulted in a fracture within this part of the cruck.

Base crucks

A three-hinged arch structure is stable against wind loads on the side of the building, but this is not so of cruck frames, where the blades are not connected together directly, and especially so with base crucks. Three timbers joined together as a base cruck form what is known as a four-bar chain (the ground being the fourth link) and would not be stable without the braces between the cruck blades and the collar. Under dead loads alone the upper part of the roof may be assumed to impose vertical loads on the base cruck structure, as shown in Figure 4.20. There

The equations describing the forces on a cruck depend upon what is measured. In practice the survey is likely to give the overall height of the structure, its span and slope of roof, and the height of the beam (Figure 4.19). The common rafters produce a load on the purlin perpendicular to the slope and horizontal and vertical loads on the wall plate. However, it is simpler to work from the external load that gives rise to these forces, i.e. W. Some of this load might be carried directly by the wall structure, as indicated by the force V', but the reaction at the purlin and the horizontal restraint of the wall plate are provided by the cruck frame. Taking moments about the foot of the cruck eliminates the force V' when:

If $T = 0$ then $Hh = Wl/4$ and $H_l = H$

If $H_l = 0$ then $H = T$ and $Wl/4 = H(h-h')$

The maximum moment will occur at the purlin, i.e. at the distance h'' below the apex, and taking moments here will give the maximum bending on the cruck blade, Hh''. The force at the apex and hence the bending moment on the cruck blade can more than double if there is no horizontal restraint at the ground.

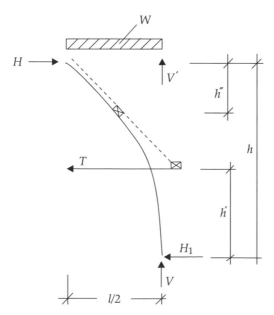

Figure 4.19 Forces on a cruck frame under dead load only.

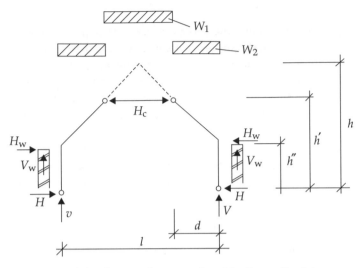

Figure 4.20 Vertical loads on a base cruck with the wall plate supported by masonry.

will then be some outward thrust at the feet of the cruck blades as a result of this, which will be greater than that for a simple cruck frame of equivalent span because the structure is lower. These outward thrusts will be transmitted via the mortice and tenon at the feet of the blades to the sole plates. Where the base cruck is raised on a masonry wall one would expect to find buttressing of the wall to resist the outward thrust of the timbers, but there is some question about the method of load transfer between the cruck blades and the masonry. The sequence of construction was for the wall to be brought up as high as the feet of the cruck blades, which would then have been raised with their feet set into sockets in the wall. It might be assumed that any outward thrust is transmitted to the wall at this point. However, in bringing up the rest of the wall the masonry could have been built round the upright part of the cruck blades. Thus any outward movement of the frame might be resisted along the whole contact surface between timber and masonry.

Drying of the timbers has been shown to produce a change in the curvature of cruck blades, and this might well induce additional forces in both the cruck frame itself and in the supporting masonry. During the framing of Pilton Barn, whose timber frame was recently rebuilt after the original was destroyed in a fire, the frames were found to change in size between the time that they were sawn out and their erection. They had moved inward because there had been an increase in the curvature

---

Calculation of the outward thrust

This calculation here is for a raised base cruck and is a little more complicated than the calculation for the ordinary cruck building because the lower roof is supported partly by the purlins and partly by the wall plate. The simplest way to handle this is to calculate the forces on the assumption that the whole of the roof is supported by the timber and then to subtract the forces at the wall plate.

In the first stage of the calculation the loads are worked out as for a timber frame wall in which the outward thrust of the lower roof will be resisted by the cruck blades, i.e. $H_w = 0$. The only vertical load from the lower part of the roof onto the cruck blades will be from the purlins. Therefore $V + V_w = W_1/2 + W_2$.

Taking moments about the foot of the blades: $H_c h' = dW_1/2 + W_2 d/2$ and $H = H_c$.

With the wall carrying the outward thrust as well as the vertical load from the wall plate, the horizontal thrust is much reduced. Again taking moments about the foot of the blade:

$$H_c h' = (W_1 + W_2)d / 2 + H_w h''$$

and

$$H = H_c - H_w$$

Values of H_w and V_w are taken from the calculations of forces at the feet of rafters as carried out above.

---

of the blades, and this was allowed for when the tenons at the feet of the blades were cut. Such a movement might be explained by the presence of reaction wood that develops in a curved member in a tree. This reaction wood has a substantial longitudinal moisture movement that would result in a change in curvature and hence the effect observed. If the timbers had been sawn out and erected immediately the feet would have been restrained by the masonry so that the effect would have been as if the span had been increased, straining the feet outward and so putting some load on the braces. As noted above, failure is commonly seen in the tenons of base cruck braces. This might be caused by tension forces resulting from wind loads or by this shrinkage movement in the cruck blades.

Finding wind forces is a complex operation. If the braces are assumed to take no tension then the structure becomes a three-hinged arch

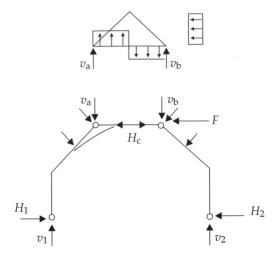

Figure 4.21 Wind loads on a base cruck.

Forces on the upper plate are found by taking moments about each plate for the horizontal and vertical components of the wind forces. These are applied to the lower part of the roof together with the total horizontal force.

Because loads on the rafters are shared between the masonry wall and the timber frame, the simplest approach is to find the forces on each slope that are resisted by the rafters and from these determine the forces at the upper plate and the purlin (Figure 4.21). These can then be applied to the free body diagram of the windward blade to find the horizontal support required from the collar as a prelude to calculating the vertical and horizontal forces at the feet of the blades.

under wind load with a hinge between the collar and the cruck blade on the windward side, while the brace on the leeward side acts in compression and braces that knee (Figure 4.21). The forces on the upper part of the roof are found first and these forces are resisted by the upper plates.

5

Loads and stresses

Having considered the general principles of load transmission in the structure it is useful to determine commonly occurring stress levels in timber frames. For this, the simple building shown in Figure 2.2 will be used, with the dimensions as shown in Figure 5.1. The calculations have been incorporated into a spreadsheet because the similar nature of many of these frames means that the basic calculations are repeated but with different dimensions. The components of the spreadsheet are distributed through the chapter, the various sections of which provide a commentary.

Rather than express weights and densities of building materials in kilogrammes and converting these to force units, the equivalent force units, i.e. newtons and kilonewtons, have been used.

Basic data

Basic data

Density, den @   8 kN/m^3

Emin @ 10 500 N/mm^2 Emean @ 13 500 N/mm^2

The density of oak is taken to be 8 kN/m^3. If deflections are to be calculated, then, assuming THA, the values of modulus of elasticity are taken to be 10 500 N/mm^2 for principal members and 13 500 N/mm^2 for load-sharing members such as rafters.[*] It will already be apparent from what has been said in the previous chapter that reliable values cannot be found for the deflections of complete frames because of the difficulty of assigning values to the properties of existing members. When deflections have been calculated for new frames, for which member

---

[*] The reader should not infer that timbers are always of THA grade. These values have been assumed simply for the example calculations.

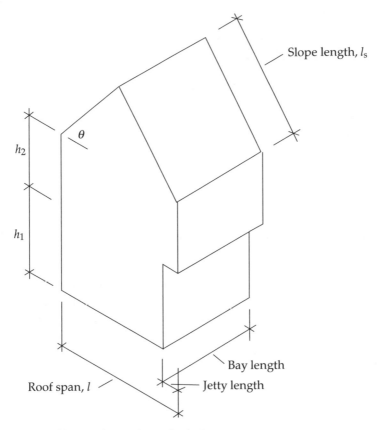

Figure 5.1 Building to be used in calculations.

properties could be assumed with reasonable confidence, they have been found to be relatively flexible compared with modern structures, and this will also be true of historic timber frames. Of course historic buildings did not have the same brittle finishes that modern structures have, nor perhaps owners so sensitive to cracks, so that larger deflections did not present a problem. Difficulties may occur if frames of this type are used in association with modern finishing materials or if they are attached to a modern structure.

Roof geometry and construction

Calculations normally start with the roof structure and the roof geometry is most simply obtained by measuring the rafter length and span so that it is useful if spread sheets for calculations are set up on this assumption. In this case with a rafter length of 4.5 m and span of 6 m, the pitch angle, $\theta = 48.2°$, which is fairly typical for roofs of this period. It is convenient to determine values for cos θ and sin θ at this stage as they will be used in subsequent calculations.

Given the dimensions and spacing of the rafters, their self-weight can be obtained as an equivalent uniformly distributed load and added to the weight of the covering and any internal lining. Originally the roof may have supported only the tiles, but in modern use insulation and some plaster ceiling is often required. This is assumed here with the overall construction comprising battens (0.034 kN/m²), roofing felt (0.01 kN/m²), 3/4" plaster (0.35 kN/m²), handmade clay tiles (0.71 kN/m²) and rafters (0.19 kN/m²). This gives a total roof load of 1.29 kN/m² measured on the slope. Machine-made tiles would be lighter and, as pointed out, the original covering of some structures might have been thatch.

From this it is convenient to calculate the total roof load/slope and the component of this perpendicular to the slope. Only long-term loads are considered for the roof timbers because the wind and snow load will produce smaller increases in stresses than that allowed for short- and medium-term loads.

Roof geometry

Roof span, l @	6 m	Slope length, l_s @	4.5 m
Rafter angle – cos θ =	0.67	sin θ =	0.75
		Pitch, θ =	48.19°

Assumed rafter sizes		rafter spacing, r_s @	405 mm
width, b @	150 mm	Depth, d @	64 mm

Roof self weight

Battens @	0.03	kN/m²
Roofing felt @	0.01	kN/m²
Plaster 0.75" @	0.35	kN/m²
Plain, handmade clay tiles @	0.71	kN/m²
Self wt of rafters b.f.	0.19	kN/m²
Total roof load, wa =	1.29	kN/m² measured on slope
Total roof load, w =	5.82	kN/m/slope
=	3.88	kN/m perpendicular to the slope

Rafter bending

While simple coupled rafter roofs were not generally used, they do, as demonstrated in the previous chapter, provide a figure for the horizontal thrust and the maximum bending moment occurring for those rafters deprived of purlin support and provide a reasonably accurate value for outward thrust on the wall plate. From the rafter dimensions given above, the load/rafter and hence the maximum bending moments and stresses on the rafters can be obtained assuming that the rafters are simply supported. In this case the bending stresses are within the limits for THA, which would not be an unreasonable assumption for fairly straight-grained coppiced timbers free from knots. If they are supported by a rigid purlin the stress will be considerably lower.

Simple coupled rafter roof

Load/rafter length =	1.57 kN – perpendicular to slope	
BM =	0.88 kN m if simply supported	
width, rb, b.f.	150 mm	Depth, rd, b.f. 64 mm
z =	0.10×10^6 mm^3	f = 8.63 N/mm^2
I =	3.28×10^6 mm^4	
EI =	44237×10^6 N mm^2	δ = 42 mm
		For a purlin roof f = 2.16 N/mm^2

These stresses may be compared with those of collar-braced rafters. If the collar is placed two-thirds up the rafter and of uniform cross-section, the forces for a range of slopes can be obtained from the figures in Table 4.1. This assumes that the feet of the rafters are free to rotate, but are effectively restrained against outward movement. The hogging bending moment at the collar is $0.042wl^2$, where l is the length of the rafter and w the load/unit length perpendicular to the rafter. The sagging bending moment halfway up the rafter is slightly higher at $0.0625wl^2$. In practice, the collar is fastened to the rafter with a half lap joint considerably reducing the bending capacity of the latter at this point, so if either of these moments is likely to be critical it will be the first. Moreover, rafters are commonly tapered towards the top, further reducing their bending capacity and also affecting these numerical results. This compares with the bending on a simple coupled rafter of $0.125wl^2$. In other words, the effect of adding a collar is to halve the bending moment. At the same time the reduction of the cross-section means that the stresses in the rafter are likely to remain much the same.

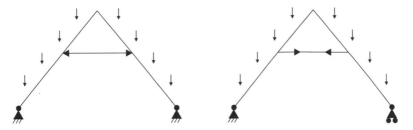

Figure 5.2 Different support conditions for collar braced rafters. These would normally be built with the feet restrained in position and the collar in compression. If the feet are free to move outward the collar will go into tension. A small amount of movement might reduce the compression in the collar without its going into tension.

<u>Collar braced roof</u>

Moment at collar =	0.45 kN m
Assuming a halved joint, z =	0.05×10^6 mm^3 $f =$ 8.70 N/mm^2

If there is outward movement of the wall plate there will be an increase in the bending moments on the rafters and a reduction in the compression force in the collar. This sometimes occurs in masonry buildings because of rotation of the wall through a combination of shallow foundations and inadequate drainage. Water running off roofs without gutters tends to weaken the soil on the outside of the building resulting in outward tilting of the wall. If the wall plate is completely unrestrained against outward movement and there are only vertical forces at the feet of the rafters there will be a considerable increase in bending moment at the collar and unacceptable resulting stresses. The force in the collar is then in tension and the forces will be many times greater (Figure 5.2).

Purlin loads and stresses

The maximum values of bending moment and stress assuming a rigid purlin, as discussed in Chapter 4, have been calculated for the roof in question assuming a bay length of 4.5 m. The purlin will have some self-weight and the component of this perpendicular to the slope has been added in to obtain the bending moment. In some cases purlins are continuous over two bays, considerably reducing the bending moment, but if it is necessary to replace part of the purlin, thus creating a pair of simply supported spans the original size might prove too small. If it is possible, placing repair splices near the points of contraflexure can go some way to reducing this effect.

Considering forces perpendicular to the plane of the roof

Bay length @	4.5 m		
load to purlin =	2.43 kN/m	total/bay =	10.92 kN
		Vertical component =	7.28 kN
purlin size width @	200 mm	Depth @	125 mm
Self wt =	0.2 kN/m		
=	0.9 kN	= (perp. to slope),	0.6 kN
		Total perpendicular to slope =	11.52 kN

$$BM = 6.48 \text{ kN m}$$
$$z = 0.52 \times 10^6 \text{ mm}^3 \qquad f = \underline{12.44 \text{ N/mm}^2}$$
$$I = 32.55 \times 10^6 \text{ mm}^4$$
$$EI = 341797 \times 10^6 \text{ N mm}^2 \qquad \delta = \underline{8 \text{ mm}}$$

With the figures used here the bending stresses are above those allowed for THB timber. They, and other primary members, will frequently contain knots and might well have some wane and/or sapwood that has suffered from beetle attack. They might well be incapable of making THA grade and the size that can be relied upon might be less than their nominal size. Under these circumstances their deflection will relieve them of some load as it is redistributed to the rafters, and this will reduce the purlin bending stresses. Some measure of the effect of deflection can be obtained by comparing the theoretical deflection of the purlin under the maximum load with the deflection of an unassisted rafter. With the sizes assumed the purlin deflection for simply supported purlins is 6 mm at mid-span, while that of the rafter is 42 mm. In other words, a purlin deflecting this amount would have shed little load from the rafters. Although the rafters would be capable of spanning unassisted, it is possible to find situations where the purlin is too small to carry the full load, and some redistribution of load back to the rafters must be assumed.

Wall plate bending

At this stage only the horizontal forces on the wall plate need be considered. It was shown that for slopes close to 45° the error involved in assuming a simple coupled rafter roof rather than a purlin roof can be ignored so that the horizontal thrust can be calculated fairly simply. For collar-braced rafters the calculations are a little more complex, but Table 4.1 gives an indication of comparative forces for the two conditions.

These figures do of course assume that the wall plate does not deflect. As it will to some extent, the actual values will be slightly lower than those obtained from the calculation. The sizes commonly used for wall plates normally result in acceptably low stresses, but it is often necessary to determine the forces involved because of the need for repairs to these members.

Load to wall plate

Horizontal thrust =	2.60 kN/m	Total/bay =	7.10 kN
BM =	6.59 kN m		
depth @	150 mm	width @	200 mm
z =	1.00×10^6 mm^3	f =	6.59 N/mm^2

> It is instructive to compare the maximum bending on a purlin with that on the wall plate. As they are the same span this can be done by comparing their relative loading. The maximum on the purlin is $(1.25W \cos \theta)/2$, while that on the wall plate is $W/2 \tan \theta$ (where W is the total load of the slope). At 45° the values of these expressions are $0.44W$ on the purlin and $0.5W$ on the wall plate. While the load on the purlin is slightly less than that on the wall plate, the former is loaded across its smaller dimension while the latter across its larger. Therefore the stresses in the wall plate are likely to be smaller than those in the purlin, even if they are the same size. In fact the wall plate is often the larger of the two.
>
> In this case the calculation of wall plate deflection has not been included because it is very small.

Lap dovetail joint

Using the diagram discussed in Chapter 3, the stresses in a lap dovetail can be found as follows:

Assume a depth of joint = d and the width of plate = a.

If the angle of joint = θ, then the length of joint = $a/\cos \theta$ and area of surfaces = $2ad/\cos \theta$.

If the allowable stress in compression across the grain = f then the maximum load that the joint can take will be $2adf \sin \theta/\cos\theta$.

In the practical example the stresses obtained from the outward thrust are within the allowable compressive stress on the timber providing there is bearing across the whole of the surfaces. In practice the effect of shrinkage is not simply to allow the wall plate to move outward because of a reduction in the width of the wall plate dovetail, but also to change the overall geometry of the joint so that the surface area in contact will be reduced (see Figure 5.3).

Angle of dovetail @	20 deg		=	0.35 rad
		force on each face of the joint =		10.38 kN
Depth of cut @	35 mm			
Length of face =	213 mm	Compressive stress =		1.39 N/mm²

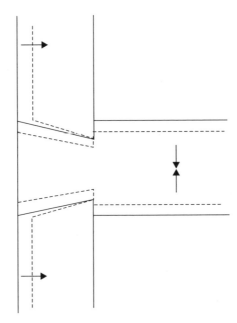

Figure 5.3 Shrinkage and change of geometry in a lap dovetail. Assuming accurate carpentry the original mating surface is shown by the solid line and the dimensions after shrinkage by the dotted lines. As the tie beam shrinks there will be a small reduction in the angle of its dovetail because of the slightly smaller dimension at the narrow end. As the wall plate shrinks there will be a much larger increase in the angle of its dovetail as shown. The result is that as the wall plate moves out to keep the two members in contact the mating surface will be reduced to a small area on the inside face of the wall plate.

Roof frames

Clasped purlin roof

In a clasped purlin roof the load is applied to the inside face of the supporting notch (see Figure 4.10) resulting in some compression in the collar. There will be modest bending in the collar, but it is normally large enough that the resulting stresses are negligibly small. Similarly, the tie beam is normally large compared with the bending stresses imposed by the load from the posts – should there be any. The problem arises when the force is to be carried by the principal rafter rather than by the posts, so that load has to be transmitted through two mortice and tenon joints. In such cases the tenon in the collar will be supporting the self-weight of the purlin plus the vertical component of the rafter thrust on the purlin. Under these two loads the upper bound value for the compressive stress on the face of the tenon may well be high compared with the allowable stress (depending upon the size of the tenon). In this example compressive stress in the tenon at an angle to the grain is compared with the allowable stress derived using Hankinson's formula.

Assuming collar and principals act to support the purlins – equal bays both sides.

Vertical component of	7.28 kN		
purlin force =			
Purlin self weight b.f.	0.90 kN	Vert. load to collar =	8.18 kN
Principal rafter force =	10.97 kN		
Tenon size width @	38 mm	length @	63 mm
		Compression stress =	4.58 N/mm²

Hankinson's formula for allowable compression in collar tenon

P@ 10.5 N/mm²		Q@	4 N/mm²
θ b.f. 48.19 deg		=	0.84 rad
		Nθ =	5.52 N/mm²

The other joint to consider is the heel joint where the principal is joined to the tie beam. Two stresses are significant here, the first being the compressive stress on the tenon. This compressive stress acts at an angle to the grain on the tenon, and Hankinson's formula for the allowable stress should be applied. However, one can see by comparing the two tenons that this will be acceptably low. The second stress which might be critical is the shear parallel to the grain in the tie beam behind the mortice in timbers possibly weakened by wetting. The area carrying the load is shown in Figure 3.3(b).

Tie beam force =	7.31 kN – horizontal component of principal rafter force		
Let tenon be: width @	32 mm	depth @	75 mm
length behind mortice	25 mm	at bottom =	100 mm
at top @			
Shear area =	12575 mm²	shear stress =	0.58 N/mm²

Load to the frames

Weight of frame

Member no	width	depth	length	
	mm	mm	m	
Principal rafters 2	125	150	4.50	0.17 m^3
collar 1	146	200	3.90	0.11 m^3
q. posts 2	160	125	0.95	0.04 m^3
tie beam 1	175	250	6.00	0.26 m^3

Total volume =	0.58 m^3
Total wt =	4.67 kN
Load from purlins =	21.94 kN
Total to be carried by two posts =	26.61 kN
=	13.30 kN/post

In calculating the load on roof frames, those most heavily loaded are the internal frames, i.e. those that carry the total load from a whole bay of the roof. For end frames these loads are halved. Occasionally unequal bays complicate the arithmetic, when it will be necessary to take half the load from each of the bays carried. From the discussion above the magnitude of this load depends upon the deflection of the purlin, so that only upper and lower bound values can be found. The upper bound values of the purlin load might be used to determine stresses within the roof frame, while the lower bound load plus the weight of the frame will provide a hold-down force that can be relied upon to resist the upward thrust of braces under wind load conditions.

For loads to the posts the weight of the frame itself must be added to that of the purlin load. The load on the front wall post will be carried by a jettied frame member at first floor level and, although it will produce some cantilever moment, these timbers are normally large enough for the resulting stresses to be comfortably small. Nevertheless, it might be a problem if this timber has to be repaired and some bending moment has to be transmitted from the new, repair timber into the original girder.

Jetty load and bending

In a two-storey building, consideration of the floor must begin with the load of the wall above the first floor to the jettied joists. This will include the weight of the wall and the load from the roof. Here a collar-braced, common-rafter roof will be assumed so that all the roof weight is carried by the walls, giving the maximum load to the structure below. This will also be an upper bound value for the load of a purlin roof. Of course, in a three-storey building this will be at the second floor with correspondingly larger forces at the first floor. The weight of the wall includes the weight of the studs and the infill, with some reduction for the windows. For the dimensions on which this is based see Figure 5.4. The calculation makes no attempt to determine the load carried by individual studs. The overall weight of the wall and roof is assumed to be delivered as a UDL to the jetty sill (or bressummer). This, like the wall plate above, is not assumed to be stiff enough to carry any significant load in bending. Hence the jettied floor joists are all assumed to carry the same load, from which it is possible to find the bending moment on the projecting joists. The weight of the wall has been found by first calculating an overall distributed weight for both the infill and the studs, assuming the latter are equally spaced.

Self-weight of wall

Height of wall, h_2 @	1.83 m			
Size of studs	width @ 200 mm		depth @	150 mm
	spacing @ 750 mm crs	Distributed weight	0.59 kN/m²	
		=		
weight of wall	Infill @ 0.79 kN/m²	allowing for studs =	1.06 kN/m	
	= 1.45 kN/m			
		Total =	7.41 kN	
Bay length b.f.	4.5 m			
Window size, ww @	1.5 m		1.20 m	
x wh @	1.20 m	Subtract window =	1.42 kN	
		load to plate allowing for window	5.98 kN	
		=		
		Load from wall plate b.f.	5.82 kN/m	
		Maximum load to jetty plate =	7.24 kN/m	

From the figures in the calculation it can be seen that the contribution of the wall to the total weight is small compared with that of the roof. Effective purlins would therefore reduce the load on the wall considerably, but increase that on the cross frames and hence on the wall posts. However, even with the full weight of the roof carried by the wall plate, and hence the wall below, the stresses in the projecting joists are relatively low. Only where joist ends have decayed and need to be replaced will the load on the jetty become an issue and determine the design of the repair joint.

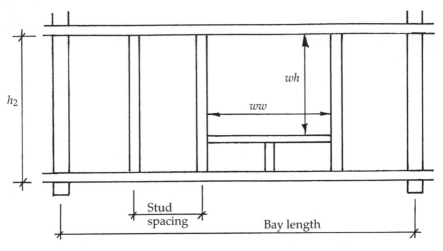

Figure 5.4 Diagram for the calculation of the weight of a wall.

Joist bending in jetty

Jetty length @	300 mm	joist spacing @	600 mm crs
Load/joist	4.29 kN		
BM/joist =	1.29 kN m		

<u>Joist size</u> width @ 125 mm depth @ 125 mm

z = 0.33×10^6 mm^3 f = <u>3.95 N/mm^2</u>

Main spans – self weight

Self wt of joists =	0.21 kN/m^2	
Allow for plaster @	0.25 kN/m^2	
Allow for 25 mm boarding =	0.2 kN/m^2	
Total =	0.66 kN/m^2	Span @ 3 m
Load/joist =	1.19 kN	
BM/joist =	0.44 kN m	f = <u>1.37 N/mm^2</u>

Main spans – live load

Live load @ 2 kN/m^2

Load/joist = 3.6 kN

BM/joist = 1.35 kN m f = 4.15 N/mm^2

f (total) = <u>5.51 N/mm^2</u>

I = 20.35×10^6 mm^4 δ = 6 mm

= $l/$ 490

Shear stress on joist tenons

Assume depth of tenon @ 38 mm Shear stress = 0.76 N/mm^2

As the stresses in the joists under self-weight alone are very low, the deflections would be similarly small and at the time these buildings were constructed the superimposed loads were probably small as well. Although modern rehabilitation work may well anticipate conversion to restaurant or similar use, calculations show that both the loads and deflections are within acceptable limits for this kind of loading.

The figures above showed that the majority of the load on the jetty was the result of the load of the roof, assuming that the purlins carry no load. If they do, the jetty load will be correspondingly reduced and the load to the spine beam increased. Therefore in calculating the stress on the spine beam it is simplest to ignore the effect of the jetty, which will reduce the load on this member. The spine beam and cross beam have been made the same size in this example to compare the stresses. The spine beam, carrying a distributed load, has relatively low stresses compared with the cross beam, with a point load at the centre. The stress in the latter is well in excess of the allowable stresses if it had to span as a simply supported beam, but in many cases these beams are assisted by the structure of partitions at ground floor level. One might also consider support being provided by braces, so reducing the effective span.

Load to spine beam

$$Floor\ load = 2.66\ kN/m^2$$
$$load\ to\ beam = 35.89\ kN$$
$$BM = 20.19\ kN\ m$$

width @	250 mm	depth @	250 mm
$z =$	$2.60 \times 10^6\ mm^3$	$f =$	7.75 N/mm²

Load to cross beam $= 35.89$ kN assuming similar bays each side
$$BM = 53.83\ kN\ m$$

width @	250 mm	depth @	250 mm
$z =$	$2.60 \times 10^6\ mm^3$	$f =$	20.67 N/mm²

In addition to the calculations presented here, the use of a building today would require a check on the fire resistance of the floor. This may be done by assuming a reduced cross-section for the timber after the required period of fire resistance (see BS 5268 Part 4). Note also that larger stresses are allowed for this condition.

Cross frames

These frames include the roof frames that have been considered above. Loads from these are transmitted down the posts and at the intermediate floor(s) the transverse beam is cantilevered to support the jetty sill. The assumption is that no wall load will be transmitted to the main transverse beam from the jetty sill, as this will all be taken by the floor joists. Just like the wall plate, it is unlikely that the jetty sill will be stiff enough to transfer loads on it back to the main frame. Therefore the only load that needs to be considered is that of the front post onto the jettied beam in case repairs are needed. Our principal concern for the cross frames is the effect of wind loading producing forces in the braces. These introduce bending moments in the posts that are unlikely to be of concern in sound timbers, but which may be a problem if repairs are required.

Wind loading and bracing

The way in which the structure resists wind loads has been described qualitatively in Chapter 4. Here we are concerned with the magnitude of the forces in the braces and the consequent bending moments on other timbers. Figure 5.5 shows the loads that are coming onto the frame. The wind loads on the roof that are actually forces perpendicular to the slopes can be simplified to a horizontal load and a moment. Wind loads on the roof are transmitted to the frame by the rafters to the purlins and wall plate, and as with dead loads the proportion of load to each is impossible to determine. Because it is the forces in the bracing that are required the simplest approach is to assume the roof to be a rigid triangular section, the loads on which can be applied to the wall plate. Wind loads on the roof surfaces produce positive pressure on the windward slope and negative pressures on the leeward slope and act halfway up each. Ignoring the vertical forces produced by this, the pressure coefficients can simply be added together and the horizontal component of loads on each bay calculated to obtain a horizontal force to be applied at wall-plate level, i.e. $qC_p l_s \sin^2 \theta \times$ bay length. To this is added the force at the wall plate generated by horizontal forces on the upper-storey wall, half of which will be transmitted to the wall plate and half to the plate at floor level. Half of the wind load on the ground floor wall will also be applied to the frame at first floor level, the other half being carried directly by the ground.

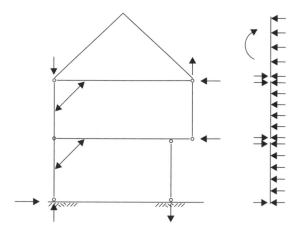

Figure 5.5 Wind loads on a frame.

Forces on roof and upper wall
Basic wind pressure, q @ 0.84 kN/m²
Force on roof
        Pressure coefficient 0.30 on windward slope
                               0.70 on leeward slope
                  Total = 1.00   Total horizontal force F_1 = 9.45 kN/bay
Forces on wall
      Height of wall, h_2 b.f. 1.83 m
        Pressure coefficient 0.70   Total horizontal force F_2 = 4.84 kN/bay
                               Load to wall plate, $F_1 + F_2/2$ = 11.87 kN/bay

The horizontal component of the wind pressures produces a moment about the wall-plate level that increases the downward force on the lee-ward post while the effect of their vertical components is to produce a larger moment in the opposite direction. Thus the hold-down force of the roof on the post-tie beam joint is reduced by the wind and it may be necessary to calculate this (see below).

Of the different bracing models discussed in Chapter 4 the simplest is that with the upper and lower storey frames treated as independent of each other. This is the most sensible one to use because of the weakness of the rear post at the floor level and has been used here. (There are occasions when there are braces only in the upper floor, so that this model might also have to be considered.) The upper floor brace resists the wind load on the wall plate while the lower brace resists both this and the wind loads delivered to the floor level. Although the cross-section is not symmetrical only one calculation has to be carried out for each floor. Once the bracing forces have been found the uplift force at the wall plate can be determined as well as the bending moments on the posts. The tie beam is usually large enough so that bending on this does not need to be considered. The uplift force must be resisted by the weight of the roof, and comparing this with the load from the roof frame one can see that the latter is smaller. This does occasionally happen, and as the roof has not failed in the past there are three possibilities: the wind forces assumed are too high; the joint has been capable of carrying tension forces; or the brace on the leeward side has carried some tension.

<u>Bracing forces in first floor frame</u>

Moment at joint =	21.72 kN m		
Bracing distance @	1.10 m	Force in brace =	19.75 kN

Uplift force at wall plate =	12.15 kN
Bending moment on column =	6.25 kN m

<u>Forces on ground floor wall</u>

Height of wall, h_1 @	1.83 m		
Pressure coefficient	0.70	Total horizontal force =	4.84 kN/bay
		load to 1st floor, Q =	16.71 kN/bay
Moment at joint =	30.59 kN m		
Bracing distance @	1.10 m	Force in brace =	27.80 kN

Bending moment on column =	8.79 kN m		
Column width @	200 mm	depth @	200 mm
z =	1.33×10^6 mm^3	f =	<u>6.59 N/mm^2</u>

The bending moments and stresses have only been calculated for the ground floor column because these will be the larger – assuming the same size of post and length of braces. Of course, if these vary more than one calculation may be necessary. The bending stresses are within acceptable limits for a sound post but might be problematic if the post needs repair.

6

Load transmission in the new carpentry

The carpentry of masonry buildings can be divided into separate elements, comprising roofs, floors and trussed partitions. The stresses in these can be assessed by considering some of the sizes recommended in the manuals of the period, although, as already noted, these do vary. Again the text of this chapter is a commentary on the calculations presented throughout, although rather than considering a single frame calculations have been carried out to compare structures of different spans. This chapter only considers the forces in the timber members and the stresses in timber joints. Loads on bolts will be considered in Chapter 7. The basic data used for subsequent calculations is as follows.

Basic data

Roof build up			Ceiling	
Slates @	0.5 kN/m²		Plaster @	0.5 kN/m²
Boarding @	0.13 kN/m²		Joists @	0.2 kN/m²
rafter@	0.23 kN/m²			
	0.85 kN/m²			0.7 kN/m²

Truss spacing @	3 m				
Roof slope @	30 deg		=	0.52 rad	
$\beta =$	30		=	0.52 rad	

Wt of roof and ceiling					
Span @ – m	6	7	8	10	12
slope length – m	3.46	4.04	4.62	5.77	6.93
Wt of one bay roof – kN/slope =	8.83	10.31	11.78	14.72	17.67
Wt of one bay ceiling – kN =	12.60	14.70	16.80	21.00	25.20

Roof trusses

The basic form of the king-post truss was robust enough to accept minor differences without any distress, so that the arrangement could be copied by carpenters with some confidence. However, structural understanding at the time was limited and there were some inappropriate uses of roof trusses, some curious modifications of the basic form and some rather poorly proportioned examples that resulted in large deflections. In spite of this the need for repair is most commonly because of decay at the eaves, requiring replacement of part of the tie beam and principal rafter. Queen-post trusses offer the opportunity to make use of attic spaces and analysis of these might need to be carried out to justify anticipated loads or as a preliminary step to the design of strengthening. The sizes recommended by contemporary manuals and those used by carpenters, which were not necessarily the same, result in low stresses in truss members, so that it is the stresses at the joints that need to be examined.

Forces in king-post trusses

In assessing the loads on the king post, the starting point, as before, is the load from the common rafters onto the purlin. In some roofs the rafters are divided at the purlin so that the estimation of load is simple. Where the rafters are continuous over the purlin they may again be treated as a two-span beam over a central support (neglecting the possible effect of deflection of the purlin). Because of the lower pitches common in these later trusses the purlins will carry much more of the load from the rafters, with the effect that the forces at the wall plate will be much lower than for the steeper pitched roofs. The purlins are then carried by the roof truss, which is where there might be difficulties of analysis and where some simplifications are useful.

The king-post truss is a statically indeterminate structure because the principal rafter is continuous and may develop some bending moments. Nevertheless, if the truss has been assembled so that the purlin is at the point where the strut props the principal rafter, and there are no deflections that would introduce bending into the principals, then we may analyse the truss as if it were pin jointed. The effect of deflections is that the principal rafter will pick up some load in bending, with a consequent reduction in the direct forces in the members. Assuming the truss is a pin-jointed frame takes no account of this

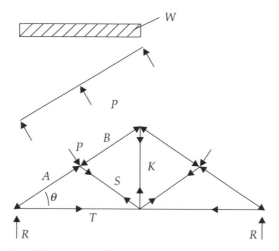

Figure 6.1 Loads and forces on a king-post truss.

bending and so must slightly overestimate the force in the struts and hence all the other axial forces – though clearly not the moments.

Figure 6.1 shows first the support reactions of the rafters perpendicular to the slope. The load W will resolve into a force $W \cos \theta$ perpendicular to the slope and an axial force in the rafters. The purlin force is, as before, $(1.25W \cos \theta)/2$. Axial forces in the rafters and the reactions at the wall plate will be taken directly by the masonry and need not be considered. Neglecting any ceiling load from the tie beam, the support reactions at the wall plate will be the vertical components of the purlin forces: $P \cos \theta$. This enables the principal rafter and tie beam forces (A and T) to be found by simply resolving the forces at the heel joint. The strut force S can be found by considering the forces perpendicular to the principal rafter (assuming that the purlin does not deflect significantly and shed load back to the rafters). At a roof slope of 45° this strut would pick up all the purlin load, but shallower pitches are more common and values have been worked out for a roof slope of 30°. The king-post force is then the sum of the vertical component of the force in each of the struts. With purlins halfway up the slope the struts meet the king post at the same angle as principal rafters, and, as there is no load applied to the head of the post, the force in both struts and at the top of the principal rafters must be the same, i.e. $S = B$. The effect of the ceiling load can then be added to these forces.

Table 6.1 puts some figures on this for a range of spans for the construction assumed. One should be aware that the truss will be required to carry a larger proportion of the roof load if there is a ridge purlin.

Span m @	6	7	8	10	12
Purlin load to frame, P =	4.78	5.58	6.38	7.97	9.56
Forces from weight of roof					
Principal rafter thrust =	8.28	9.66	11.04	13.80	16.56
Tie beam force =	7.17	8.37	9.56	11.95	14.34
Strut force =	5.52	6.44	7.36	9.20	11.04
King post load, kN =	5.52	6.44	7.36	9.20	11.04
Forces from weight of ceiling					
Ceiling load to K post =	6.30	7.35	8.40	10.50	12.60
Principal rafter thrust =	6.30	7.35	8.40	10.50	12.60
Tie beam force =	5.46	6.37	7.27	9.09	10.91
Total forces					
King post load, kN =	11.82	13.79	15.76	19.70	23.64
Principal rafter thrust =	14.58	17.01	19.44	24.30	29.16
Tie beam force =	12.63	14.73	16.84	21.05	25.26
Total load to wall plate =	10.44	12.18	13.92	17.40	20.88

Table 6.1 King-post truss.

Also, if small scantling purlins are used, rather than common rafters and purlin, the principal rafter will be acting as a two-span beam supported in the same way as the rafter discussed in Chapter 4 (Figure 4.7). This support will involve larger axial forces in the principals and correspondingly larger forces at the heel joint and in the tie beam. These forces will be more than double the values given in Table 6.1.

The load of the ceiling can now be added in, and this is normally supported by joists that are either carried directly by the tie beam or, for vaulted ceilings, hung from it. Assuming that the tie beam is in two lengths joined close to the king post, it will act as two simply supported beams, so that the load carried by the metal straps to the king post will be approximately half of the ceiling weight. The figures used in the calculation assume a roof of slates over boarding, which was common at the time, and a plaster ceiling. Trusses are assumed to be at 10 ft (3 m) spacing and the forces in the members have been calculated for spans varying between 20 ft (6 m) and 40 ft (12 m), although at these larger spans it would be more usual to have two pairs of purlins and additional strutting.

Inspection of the results (Table 6.1) shows that contribution to the king post load from the weight of the ceiling is, for the figures assumed, not insignificant, although it has a relatively smaller effect on the principal rafter and tie beam forces. The accuracy of the results will be affected by any deflection of the purlins, by drying shrinkage in the timbers and by any inaccuracy in the carpentry. Curiously, there was a period when it was recommended that the king post of the truss should be made of oak even though the rest of the members were made of softwood. It is true that the king post carries large compression forces across the grain, so a strong timber like oak might be advisable, but oak has a greater drying shrinkage than the softwood alternative and was likely to have been at a higher moisture content when used. Shrinkage of an oak king post by 5% in a post of 12" (300 mm) would result in a movement of about ½" (12 mm) across its width. This would be the equivalent of increasing the distance between the heel joint and the king post by ¼" (6 mm) each side. In a 30° roof the king post would be allowed to drop by about ½" (12 mm) as there was rotation of the principal rafters to take up this shrinkage. More significantly, the joggle at the foot of the king post would also shrink a similar amount, allowing the struts to move inward. This would allow deflection in the principal rafters, with some resulting bending stress in them. Of course, it is not the forces in the members that is significant but the stresses that these generate. However, before considering the stresses in the king-post truss it is useful to compare the forces in it with those in a queen-post truss.

Queen-post truss

While the queen-post truss provides greater support to the roof and the ceiling and has shorter members than a king-post truss of the same span, the additional support means that more load is carried by the trusses rather than going directly to the wall plate. (The same is true of a longer spanning king-post truss that carries two pairs of purlins.) A basic queen-post truss has been assumed with two pairs of purlins with the same spans and roof pitch as the king-post truss, so that the two can be compared. To determine the purlin loads the rafters can be treated as beams spanning continuously over two intermediate supports providing the spans and loads equal $P = (1.1W \cos \theta)/3$. Again it has been assumed that load from the purlins acts perpendicular to the plane of the roof with loads applied at the top of the queen post and halfway along the principals (Figure 6.2).

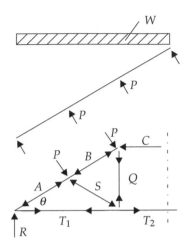

Figure 6.2 Loads and forces on a queen-post truss.

One force is delivered by the strut to the foot of the queen post, and another to the top of the queen post. The forces in the struts, and hence the posts, are naturally smaller than those in a basic king-post truss of the same span. As the purlins pick up a larger proportion of the total roof load, the forces in the principal rafters and tie beam are correspondingly larger. In fact, there is an increase of almost 25% in the forces in these members. The advantage of separating out the forces produced by the roof load from those produced by the ceiling is that the effect of a floor within the roof space can easily be seen. Naturally this produces a considerable increase in the forces in the truss, especially in the queen posts. If a floor load of $2\,\text{kN/m}^2$ is assumed across just the central third of the tie beam, i.e. between the posts, then the resulting forces in the members can be determined (see Table 6.2).

Forces at joints

The stresses in a typical roof can be assessed for the recommended sizes given in early carpenters' manuals, for which the stresses within the members are low compared with those allowed by modern codes. This is even so for the bending stresses in a loaded tie beam, although these have not been calculated because sizes found in practice vary considerably. The forces at the joints can most usefully be considered at the heel joint – the most heavily stressed in these trusses. Rather than calculate the stresses for all the spans, a typical joint has been considered and the

Span, m @	6	7	8	10	12
Purlin load to frame, P =	2.81	3.27	3.74	4.68	5.61
Forces from weight of roof					
Principal rafter thrust =	9.72	11.34	12.96	16.19	19.43
Tie beam force at wall plate =	8.42	9.82	11.22	14.03	16.83
Strut force =	3.24	3.78	4.32	5.40	6.48
Central tie force =	5.61	6.55	7.48	9.35	11.22
Queen post force =	1.62	1.89	2.16	2.70	3.24
Upper principal rafter force =	8.10	9.45	10.80	13.50	16.19
Collar force =	8.42	9.82	11.22	14.03	16.83

Forces from weight of ceiling

Ceiling load to Q post =	4.2	4.9	5.6	7	8.4
Principal rafter load =	8.4	9.8	11.2	14	16.8
Collar and tie force =	7.27	8.49	9.70	12.12	14.55

Total forces

Principal rafter thrust =	18.12	21.14	24.16	30.19	36.23
Tie beam force at wall plate =	15.69	18.30	20.92	26.15	31.38
Central tie force =	12.88	15.03	17.18	21.47	25.77
Queen post force =	5.82	6.79	7.76	9.70	11.64
Upper principal rafter force =	16.50	19.25	22.00	27.50	32.99
Collar force =	15.69	18.30	20.92	26.15	31.38

With floor

Forces from a floor over the central part of the truss   Floor load @ 2 kN/sq m

Floor load to Q post =	6	7	8	10	12
Principal rafter load =	12	14	16	20	24
Collar and tie force =	10.39	12.12	13.86	17.32	20.78

Total forces

Principal rafter thrust =	30.12	25.34	28.96	36.19	43.43
Tie beam force at wall plate =	26.08	21.94	25.08	31.35	37.61
Central tie force =	23.28	18.67	21.34	26.67	32.00
Queen post force =	11.82	8.89	10.16	12.70	15.24
Upper principal rafter force =	28.50	23.45	26.80	33.50	40.19
Collar force =	26.08	21.94	25.08	31.35	37.61

Table 6.2 Queen-post truss.

maximum force that it will carry calculated from the allowable stresses. Considering the force on the end of the tenon at the heel joint and applying Hankinson's formula the maximum allowable stress at 30° to the grain is a little over 5 N/mm². With the size of joint assumed the maximum tensile force in the tie beam is just over 12 kN, a force that is exceeded in a king-post truss of only 6 m span that is carrying a ceiling. The problem is worse in queen-post trusses or more complex king-post trusses carrying two pairs of purlins, which will both have larger forces. Therefore it is difficult to justify carpentry joints used in repairs, and a similar problem will be encountered when alterations are made putting attics with queen-post trusses into use.

The shear in the short-grain timber behind the mortice (or bridle) also needs to be considered. The areas required to resist this have been calculated for the maximum allowable force on each joint. The advantage of the nineteenth century shift to the use of bridle joints can be readily seen. With a bridle joint of the same depth a considerably larger area of bearing could be achieved, with a consequent increase in the allowable load on the joint. With the dimensions suggested the joint is capable of carrying the forces generated by a long-spanning queen-post truss with a floor load.

Forces at joints

<u>Hankinson's formula</u>   To find the maximum allowable stress for 'fir' at an angle to the grain.

P @	7.9 N/mm²	Q @	2.4 N/mm²
θ @	30 deg	=	0.52 rad
Nθ =	5.02 N/mm²	Assuming C24 softwood	

<u>Mortice and tenon at the heel joint</u>

Assume tenon is	1.5 in	×	2.5 in
	38 mm		64 mm
Maximum force =	12.15 kN		

Considering the timber in shear behind the mortice

@   2.00 N/mm²   6076 mm² is required

<u>Bridle joint</u>

Assume bridle width @	4	×	2.5 in
	102 mm		64 mm
Maximum force =	32.40 kN		

Considering the timber in shear behind the joint

@   2.00 N/mm²   16202 mm² is required

In roofs where the principal rafter is set back from the wall plate to accommodate a box gutter the principal rafter force will introduce some bending in the tie beam. This is unlikely to be a significant bending stress on the original tie beam, but it might well be in any repair because it will have to be resisted by the joint between new and existing timber if a new tie beam end is required.

A significant difference between the basic king and queen post forms is that the struts on the former produce equal and opposite forces on the foot of the post, whereas there is a force on only one side of the foot of a queen post. Using the forces obtained for the queen-post truss assumed above and assuming that the tenon is 1.5 in × 2.5 in (38 × 64 mm) the stresses on the side of the tenon can be calculated. These need to be compared with an allowable compressive stress perpendicular to the grain of 2.4 N/mm². They are acceptable for the truss designs assumed, but it is possible to imagine designs where the allowable load would be exceeded. While trusses were built with the queen posts notched into the tie beam or with a timber added between the feet of the queen posts to take this force, in repairing a long-span truss it might be necessary to add supplementary steel angles between the post and the tie beam.

Q post – lower tenon

Span @ – m	6	7	8	10	12
strut force b.f., kN	3.24	3.78	4.32	5.40	6.48
Horizontal component =	2.81	3.27	3.74	4.68	5.61
Assume tenon is	1.5 in	x		2.5 in	
	38 mm			64 mm	
Stress, N/mm² =	1.16	1.35	1.55	1.93	2.32

The other joint that needs to be considered is that at the foot of the posts where the tie beam is supported. An indication of the magnitude of the force to be carried is provided by the value of the ceiling loads to the king and queen posts in Tables 6.1 and 6.2. These would be carried first by the strap round the tie beam and then through the bolts through the posts. No evidence of distress has been seen in these fastenings and they appear generally to come within the limits for bolt loads given in the code of practice. The 19th century practice of using pairs of timbers for the king and queen posts that clasped the principal rafters and tie beams of the truss (Figure 3.18) seems to have been a retrograde step. This simplified the carpentry but meant that forces in the posts were transmitted across the rather small shoulders into the other members by stresses across the grain. The detail illustrated is from a roof by Robert Smirke with a span of 62' 7" (19 m) that carried a heavy coffered plaster ceiling as well as the roof covering, and some crushing of the timber was noted where the hardwood posts clasped the softwood of the other members.

Raised tie beam truss

Raised tie beam trusses were used where a ceiling rose above the level of the wall plate and their construction, illustrated by Price, clearly shows that their ties were assumed to be in tension. The inclined hammerbeams were set under the feet of the principal rafters and were bolted to the tie at its centre in order to carry tension forces. But the tie was also strapped at its ends to the principals, suggesting that it too was seen as carrying tension forces. The truss illustrated in Figure 6.3 is taken from one shown by Price, and although he does not show the purlin positions, these seem reasonable. The purlin loads will be as for the queen-post truss. If the hammerbeams do nothing then the truss is reduced to the form shown in Figure 6.3(b). There are large compression and bending forces in the principal rafters and a correspondingly large tension force in the tie that will have to be carried by bolts and straps.

	Collar @ h/3			$\beta =$	0.19 rad
				$\theta - \beta =$	0.33 rad
Span @ – m	6	7	8	10	12
slope length – m	3.46	4.04	4.62	5.77	6.93
Load, truss/slope, kN	8.83	10.31	11.78	14.72	17.67
Purlin load, kN =	2.81	3.27	3.74	4.68	5.61
R =	6.48	7.56	8.64	10.80	12.96

Assuming no restraint by hammerbeams

	Principal rafter forces and moments				
Compressive force in	12.96	3.27	3.74	4.68	5.61
principal =					
BM, kN m =	6.48	3.82	4.99	7.79	11.22
Tie force, kN =	8.42	9.82	11.22	14.03	16.83
If the hammerbeam is fully effective					
Tension force, kN =	17.14	20.00	22.85	28.56	34.28

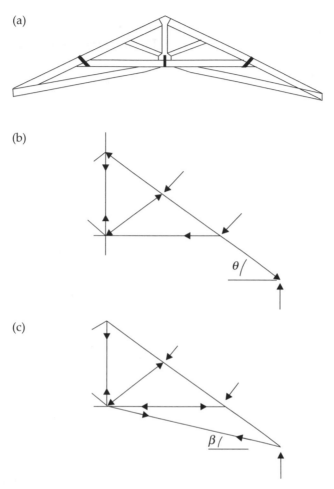

Figure 6.3 Loads and forces on a raised tie beam truss (a). Two extreme cases are considered in which the hammerbeams are either completely ineffective (b) or carry the whole of the tie force (c).

If, in contrast, we assume that the hammerbeams are totally effective as ties, then the forces in the truss are as shown in Figure 6.3(c). The 'tie beam' will be in compression, just as the collar of collar-braced rafters must be in compression. This is statically indeterminate unless a pin is assumed at the collar/rafter joint, when the tie force in the hammer-beams can be found by taking moments about this joint. The result is very large forces in the hammerbeams, but only assuming no slippage of the bolts at the centre of the tie. It seems more likely that there would, in practice, be considerable slippage of these fasteners. It also seems unlikely that there would be sufficient slippage for the tie to be acting alone without any assistance from the hammerbeams as considered above. In practice it will be necessary to examine the truss to determine a likely mode of behaviour, possibly carrying out a full elastic analysis as a starting point.

Floors

Publishing first in 1733, Francis Price provided tables of scantlings for both large and small buildings and for both oak and fir, so that the simplest way of assessing a typical floor of the period is to take sizes from his tables, making some assumptions about the loads. Assuming for example a modern design load for domestic use of 1.5 kN/m^2 and that the joints are 12" (305 mm) apart (Table 6.3), then the stresses are less than 2 N/mm^2, even for spans of 12 ft (3.65 m), and the deflections are negligible. The sizes used for this calculation are those given for small buildings. Those for large buildings, and thus presumably of better quality, are larger, so the stresses will be even smaller for the same loading.

If the same exercise is carried out for girders a slightly different picture emerges (see Table 6.4). The assumption here is that girders are at the equivalent of 10 ft (3 m) centres and carry the same overall loading. The stresses are still well within acceptable limits, but the deflections for fir members are beginning to approach that allowed today, and this is before any allowance has been made for the self-weight of the floor and the ceiling load. William Pain, about half a century later, published several books, and his tables differ. He makes no distinction between oak and fir. Overall the stresses in his joists are slightly higher than for sizes recommended by Price, while those for his girders are lower and they are correspondingly stiffer. One might assume that carpenters were gaining in experience, but the sizes actually used were not always those given in any of the tables. Indeed, very similar houses built in the same street sometimes have differently sized floor timbers. Presumably builders were influenced by what timber was available.

Nineteenth century writers, such as Tredgold (1820) and Newlands (c1850) chose to substitute formulae for the 18th century tables. The formula used was to take the square of the span in feet and divide by the breadth of the member in inches. The cube root of the quotient was then to be multiplied by a factor that depended upon the material and

Joist spacing @		12 in = 305 mm		Load @ 1.5 N/m²		
	Fir				*Oak*	
	E (fir) @		10800 N/sq.mm	E (oak) @		12000 N/sq mm
span (ft)	depth (in)	width (in)	f (N/mm²)	depth (in)	width (in)	f (N/mm²)
6	5	2.5	1.12	5	3	0.93
9	6.5	2.5	1.49	7.5	3	0.93
12	8	2.5	1.75	10	3	0.93

Table 6.3 Common joists for small buildings – from Francis Price (1733).

	Spacing @		3 m		Load @ 1.5 N/m²	
	E (fir) @		7200 N/mm²			
fir – span (ft)	depth (in)	width (in)	f (N/mm²)	δ (mm)	l/δ	
16	11	8	5.06	12	391	
20	12.5	10	4.90	17	367	
24	14	12	4.69	20	359	
oak – span	E (oak) @		7500 N/mm²			
16	13	10	2.90	6	841	
20	14	12	3.25	9	645	
24	15	14	3.50	14	536	

Table 6.4 Girders for small buildings – from Francis Price (1733).

whether the member was a joist or a girder. Again if joists are assumed to be at 12 in (305 mm) centres and girders at 10 ft (3 m) centres, very low stresses and small deflections are obtained for 2.5 in (63 mm) wide joists and 10 in (254 mm) wide girders. But loads are not discussed in relation to these design rules, so that, if anything, the factors for girders seem a little too small compared with those for joists, because we might expect the longer girders to be used in commercial premises with higher loads.

We might compare the sizes recommended here with a building of the period. Kimmings Mill, a flour mill in Stroud. has joists spanning 10 ft (3 m) measuring 3" × 7" (76 mm × 178 mm) and main beams (or girders) of 12 ft (3.66 m) span measuring 13" × 13" (330 mm × 330 mm). As a mill we would today expect the design load to be 5 kN/m². and this results in fairly low stresses and deflections.

Kimmings Mill

| | Spacing of joists @ | 0.3 m | | load @ | 5.00 | kN/m² |
| | E (min) @ | 7200 N/mm² | | E (mean) @ | 10800 | N/mm² |

	span	depth	width	BM	z (in³)	f	δ
	(ft)	(in)	(in)	(kN m)	(x 10⁶ mm³)	(N/ mm²)	(mm)
Joists	10	7	3	1.74	0.40	4.34	4
Girders	12	13	13	25.49	6.00	4.25	5

Building regulations of the late 19th century did not always specify the sizes of floor timbers. These were not included in the Model By-laws because it was felt that local authorities might not have sufficient inspectors to enforce such a regulation. Nevertheless, some cities did specify timber sizes, including Liverpool, where separate sizes were given for domestic structures and warehouses. Examination of these suggests that while adequate for the shorter spans, the longer spans of both joists and girders might not satisfy present-day codes for warehouse loading.

Buildings of the 18th and 19th centuries may well have been designed as commercial or industrial premises and so have had heavy loads from the beginning, but it is also common to convert what were originally domestic premises to office or other commercial use. The closeness of such buildings to city centres makes this an attractive proposition, but can present a problem with floor loads. The sizes of the spaces in buildings of this date can suggest excessive bending stresses and deflections if present-day design loads are used to obtain building regulation approvals. Moreover, such loads could also have an effect on the apparent adequacy of trussed partitions that are carrying the floors. English Heritage (1996) has recognised this problem and suggested that it is unreasonable to apply the design loading of 5 kN/m² suggested by the British Standard. If storage spaces are required then they should be sensibly located where strengthening of the structure is not required. Otherwise the 'actual loading which the occupants of offices, their furniture, and storage put upon the floor will rarely exceed the loading from domestic occupation'.

Another approach to this is to consider how much of the design load of the floor is really a long-term load. Illustrations to the EH advisory leaflet cited above show offices that do contain large desks, filing cabinets and plan chests, all heavy items of furniture that will be a permanent load. But there are other uses where the design load can be high but where it is unlikely to be permanent. Classrooms and restaurants require a larger than domestic design load, but this is clearly not permanent, the load on the latter being only a few hours each day. In their first edition Ozelton and Baird (1976: 39) note that the codes give 'no guidance on the design permanence of an imposed load, the implications with regard to the design of timber structures not being recognised'. They go on to note that the Swedish building code distinguishes between 'permanent imposed' and 'live imposed' for floors, with the former being 1/3 of the total. This seems to be a sensible basis for the assessment of floors and their supporting timber structures in rehabilitation work.*

Trussed partitions

It is difficult to make any general comments about the analysis of trussed partitions and the kinds of repairs that might be wanted. This is because of both the variety of arrangements used and the kinds of alterations that might have been made. The original design or the construction of the partitions might well have been poor, resulting in large deflections of the partition and hence the floors that it supports, but without some opening up of the structure it will not be possible to diagnose the causes of any signs of distress. Analysis of this kind of truss might also be difficult because of the tendency to divide the partition into two zones, one above the door heads and one below. In some cases it is quite clear that the load is carried entirely by the trussing above the door heads. This might have the disadvantage of larger forces in the members, and hence larger stresses at the joints, but has the advantage that the structure is less likely to be compromised by subsequent alterations. Where there is trussing in both zones it might not always be clear how the load is shared between the two sets of trussing. In some cases loads on the bottom plate of the truss are transferred to the top

---

* A survey of office floor loading some 30 years ago by Mitchell and Woodgate (1971) seems to have had little influence on the code of practice for loading. The survey measured the permanent imposed loads and the results showed that the design loads required by the code were at the upper end of a long tail in the distribution curve of actual loads. This supports the view that the required loads are unreasonably high for the kinds of office that would occupy refurbished historic buildings. More recently, Alexander (2002) has reviewed the position of the codes with respect to office floor loads. He finds quite different characteristic loads for upper floors (3.5 kN/m²) and those at or below ground floor level (4.5 kN/m²).

plate by means of long iron rods, although carpenters' manuals suggest the use of simple metal straps to connect the timbers.

The original drawing of the truss shown in Figure 2.18 was labelled 'Trussed partition over the Hall' and spanned as indicated 27' 10" (8.48 m). It was produced by Timothy Lightoler for Stoneleigh Abbey, although it is not known whether this partition was actually built. The partition divided rooms from a passage and the dotted line on the drawing refers to an intersecting partition behind, thus dividing that space into two rooms. The dimensions of the timbers were also marked on the drawing as follows:

A: the beam 12 inches square
B: King pieces 6 inches by 4½ and the heads joggled
C: Counter Beam 8 inches deep by 4½
D: Framing joyst (sic) that may be sized at pleasure
E: Bressummer 6 inches by 4½
F: Counter King posts 6 inches by 4½
G: principal Braces 8 inches by 4½

This drawing is a rare survivor from the 18th century and that it was dimensioned in this way shows that the importance of the truss was recognised.

It is clear that it is the queen-post truss whose tie beam forms the door lintels that should be doing all the work. The trussing beside the doors with the so-called king pieces B can do nothing. The only purpose of this framing would have been to support the tie beam C during construction, while the members B are serving as ties to transmit floor load to the trussing above – trussing that seems rather ill proportioned for the considerable load that it might have to carry. If either the trussing fails or the tie straps prove to be less than fully effective, load will be thrown onto the beam A. Of course if the trussing fails to act as it should the braces under the joggles of the posts B might well pick up load. In that case load would be delivered to the beam A at the feet of the posts F. One might well imagine load from the floor at the lower level being carried as a UDL by the beam with two point loads at F from the floor above.

7

Decay and repair

Although this chapter deals with the structural aspect of repairs, the design of repairs to historic fabric does not depend upon structural considerations alone. In many cases there will be issues of historic value or simply visual appearance that also need to be considered, so that the repair method adopted might not always be the most structurally efficient. As well as providing an adequate structure, the conservator may be concerned with issues of reversibility, with the maximum retention of historic material and with the overall conservation philosophy that might restrict the range of repair options available. For example, dismantling of the structure for repair in the workshop is possible with some types of structure and might allow the use of repair techniques that would be impossible for *in situ* repair. However, either total or partial dismantling of a structure risks further damage and will result in a possibly unacceptable loss of secondary material.

There are many situations where an existing building is to be given a new lease of life and where the work required goes beyond simply the repair of damage or decay. It may well be that the structure was poorly designed initially so that damage has occurred because joints or members have been frequently overloaded, or that the structure has been altered in the past in such a way that its structural integrity has been compromised. In such cases the problem is not simply to repair the damage but to strengthen the structure so that it is able to carry loads safely and without further distress. If the original design was inadequate this raises a basic problem in the philosophy of repair. Should one seek to make the existing structural arrangement work or should one change the structure to one that would work better? A third possibility is to introduce new structure. In some cases the changes made to the structure in order to ensure its continuing survival might be quite radical. Consider the following example.

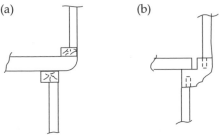

Figure 7.1 (a) The normal arrangement for jettied construction and (b) the unusual detail found in an early seventeenth century building.

A three-storey building was jettied at second floor level. The normal structural arrangement is as shown in Figure 7.1(a), in which the jettying floor joists act as cantilevers to support the bressummer and hence the wall above. In this case it was as shown in Figure 7.1(b), with a single timber forming both the head plate of the first floor wall and the bressummer supporting the second floor wall. (This is essentially a window sill detail.) In this case the moment produced by the forces from the second floor wall being in front of the first floor wall was being carried by the bressummer back to the tenons in the top of the first floor wall studs, which were therefore having to act in bending. The studs had clearly been capable of carrying this, except that decay in the bressummer was now calling into question its ability to transfer the load. Moreover, the condition of the stud tenons into the bressummer that had to be capable of transmitting the necessary bending moments could not easily be investigated, so it was impossible to guarantee their continuing structural adequacy. A further complication was that the wall had moved outward because of this poor structural arrangement to an extent that some floor joists had almost no bearing, and it was clearly necessary to provide some restraint against further movement.

In this case the most satisfactory approach to repair was to change the structural behaviour to the more normal sequence of load transfer. This was done by introducing steel brackets between the second floor wall studs and the second floor joists to transmit the forces, thus by-passing the bressummer. Once this was carried out it was possible to cut out and replace decayed parts at the front of the bressummer without having to worry about possible loading on it. In this case it was simply decay that had raised concerns about the structure and the need to replace decayed timber. In cases where there have been historically significant changes that have compromised the structure it may not be possible to reconcile retaining the changed form while ensuring a sound structure.

One possibility that always needs to be considered is that the structural action today is not that when the building was first constructed and might not be one that could be justified by modern engineering principles. It has already been pointed out that creep deflection and shrinkage of the timbers will cause some redistribution of load. Deterioration of the structure can have a far more severe effect on the load path within the building. It often seems that there is some kind of force of habit by which buildings continue to stand long after any rational assessment of the structure suggests that they should have either collapsed or at least shown signs of extreme distress. Roof trusses have sometimes been found that are completely unsupported by the posts below them because of beetle infestation of the top of the post. That they have not shown signs of distress can only be explained by changes in the load path, although exactly how one might not be able to determine. This will be discussed again below and in Chapter 8, but it is clear in such circumstances that the engineer will have to provide a structure that can be justified. This might seem irrational to a client or an architect who is being advised to introduce structure where there was none before and for which there seems no obvious need. Sometimes the conservation engineer will need to explain to the client or the architect the need for structural intervention. An ability to communicate structural ideas clearly and simply is therefore a skill worth developing.

Classification of repairs

It is useful to attempt some classification of repairs to identify the issues that need to be considered in design. For our purposes here repairs can be classified into:

(1) Those where timber is replaced with timber. In such cases the repair might be effected with carpentry alone, although the 'carpentry' of structural repairs usually requires some kind of mechanical fastening. Therefore the term 'carpentry' is used here to refer to both 'pure' carpentry with no metal fasteners and carpentry that does use these devices, which are effectively the modern equivalent of the medieval peg or the 18th century bolt and stap. The most common situations are where repairs are at decayed or damaged joints, or where a decayed end or face is to be replaced. In the first kind their function is simply to transmit forces to the remainder of a member. In the second the repaired

member must be capable of carrying the bending and shear loads.

(2) Those where timber is supplemented with some other material, either a steel plate, carbon fibre or some other reinforcing material. These are usually for the simple strengthening of a member that has inadequate load-carrying capacity, but may also be used to connect new timber to old, where part of a member has to be replaced.

(3) Those where steel or some other material is used to replace the timber. Such repairs are most often used where there are decayed ends of floor beams or tie beams and principal rafters of roofs. They have the advantage that less historic material is lost, if this is a consideration, but can usually only be used if the appearance of the repair is not of concern. There are occasions when such a repair might be designed as a visual complement to 'cradle' some valuable timber component, such as a precious decorative beam, but such instances are unusual.

(4) The use of supplementary structures that act either independently of the original, simply providing it with support, or which act in consort with the original structure although altering its structural behaviour. Such supplementary structure could either be of timber or steel.

Design codes

Present-day design codes are intended for the design of modern structures and not for the analysis and repair of historic structures. This affects the way in which timber properties are specified, the kinds of structural connections that are considered within the codes and the range of timber fasteners dealt with. The position at the time of writing is that the British Standard for structural timber, BS 5268, is to be replaced by Eurocode 5 (EC5), and these two codes are based on quite different approaches to design. The former is an 'old-fashioned' code depending upon limiting allowable stresses, while the latter is a limit-state code (as are those for other structural materials).* However, the method for determining allowable fastener loads in BS 5268 already anticipates that in EC5.

---

* Some would say that a stress limit code is more appropriate to timber, while others deprecate the delay in moving to a limit state code for this material.

BS 5268 was never completely satisfactory as a code for conservators. Its original 1984 edition failed to cover oak as a structural material, although this was changed in the 1996 edition. Neither give tabulated loads for the sizes of coach screw commonly used by conservators, but, as the present edition provides the formulae from which tabulated loads have been derived, allowable loads can be calculated for any size and length of fastener. The 2002 edition of the code extended the sizes of screws covered and corrected the table of bolts for hardwoods.[†] At present we are in a transitional period with a recently issued edition of BS 5268, even though we anticipate a change to EC5. This means that most engineers will continue to use BS 5268 for a while and the use of this code has been assumed. It is also worth noting that as the present code is still based on limiting working stresses the superseded but still current stress limit code (BS 449) remains appropriate for the design of any supplementary steelwork.

Because codes are developed for today's designs it is essential to take a wider view than simply relying upon them completely. Their limitations should be recognised and recourse might have to be made to other sources such as the English Heritage recommendations for floor loads (English Heritage, 1996). An analysis of the deflections of historic timber frames shows that they are likely to be larger than those accepted within modern codes, but as the finishes used are less brittle this need not be a problem. Some engineers seem to have been reluctant to use sizes of coach screws larger than those covered by BS 5268, in spite of the advantages that they give over bolts. The way to cope with many of these problems is to return to earlier codes, to look at some of the experimental results upon which they were based or to use the formulae provided in the present code.

Timber for repair

Moisture content

In making repairs the carpenter will need to obtain timbers of the necessary species and grade, and possibly of the correct moisture content. Timbers of the same species as the original will have the same appearance and will have the same moisture movement characteristics. The last will mean that in-service changes in moisture content will not

---

† The table in the 1996 edition did not agree with the results that could be obtained by applying the formulae given.

result in differential movement of the two, although relative movement does need to be considered in the initial drying out phase. Repairs are normally made to timbers that are dry, or at least relatively so compared with the moisture content of freshly felled timber. An apparent convention for specifying green oak for repairs to timber-framed structures has no obvious logic except that the timber will be easier to work. Using timbers that are green has implications for both the subsequent appearance of a repair and its structural design because of the shrinkage that will occur. It would be preferable to have the repair material at much the same moisture content as the original timber in order to minimise relative movement between them, but this is not always possible. It may be easy to manage with small repairs, where dried timber can be obtained, but is seldom possible for large structural sections because of the time that these take to dry. The result is that some movement of the timbers is to be expected after the repairs have been made and the carpenter might wish to allow for this in sizing the repair timbers. It is essential to consider such effects on a repair as the splitting of new wood if it dries while being constrained by two lines of fasteners.

Where moisture movement is critical it may be possible to condition smaller sections of timber by bringing them to the site well before use. In this way they can be conditioned at the relative humidity that they will experience in service and so will dry to the correct moisture content. Of course this does imply sufficiently advanced purchase and enough room on the site to store them, a counsel of perfection that will seldom be possible in practice. If large sections are required and it is particularly important to control moisture movement, laminated timber can be used. The timber is sawn into small sections, dried down to the required moisture content and then glued together to make up the required section. Of course the result will be visible if exposed, but this device might be adopted where the original surface is to be retained because of some decorative feature. If this is to be glued back to the structural section it conceals the new wood.

Structural aspects of the design of joints when using green timber will be discussed below, but there are also a number of non-structural aspects of repairs where moisture movement might affect their design. For example, cupping could result in opening up of the joints between the new timber and the old, so the former needs to be placed to avoid this. It should be placed so that the cupping is downward toward the original timber. If it cups upward and away from the original material the joint along the sides of the repair will open up. In some cases it is desirable to use timbers slightly larger than the original and to plane down to size. However, selection can be based on more than just matching moisture content and could include direction or grain or even surface checks within the timber.

Structural grade

The general grading of structural timbers was discussed in Chapter 1, but some additional comments are useful for the design of repairs. The allowable stresses used for compression across the grain should usually be those for when wane is not allowed, as that will be the condition in the vast majority of repairs. While a piece of timber might be supplied to THB or GS grade it is its strength at the repair or the strength of the piece that is cut from it that is important. This has already been discussed in Chapter 1, but when the piece used in repair is only part of the cross-section of the graded timber the relationship of any knot to the cross-section will be changed. An edge knot might be eliminated altogether in the cutting of the timber, while a face knot might become an arris knot. Of course the carpenter is likely to avoid the latter, but this does raise issues of effective use of the material and of quality assurance.

If a timber is cut down to provide a section to be used in the refacing of a member – a not uncommon requirement in the repair of timber frame buildings – then that timber may well be called upon to carry bending moments. If that section contains a knot then the size of the knot will have become a larger proportion of the cross-section of the timber, suggesting that some regrading is required. Because this may not be practicable some guidance is appropriate on what constitutes good practice in the selection and cutting of such timbers where their load-carrying performance is important.

(1) Sections with face knots may be reduced in cross-section providing there is no reduction in the width of the face in which the knot occurs.
(2) Margin knots may be cut off.
(3) Margin and splay knots – only the width containing the longer part of the knot may be reduced.
(4) The effect of cutting arris knots may vary considerably and it is difficult to form a general rule. There should certainly be no reduction that does not eliminate or cut through this type of knot, because otherwise its size would increase in proportion to the overall cross-section.

For a definition of these terms see Appendix 2.

Fasteners

The most commonly used fasteners in repair work are bolts and coach screws (normally 10 mm or 12 mm diameter) and these need to be discussed in some detail. Of the two the more useful are coach screws. Until the 1996 edition of the code, allowable loads for screws were based upon experimental work carried out in the United States and summarised in *Wood Handbook* (Forest Products Laboratory, 1974). In the earliest British code for timber (CP112) allowable loads for fasteners were given for groups of species and not for individual species. The groups used for joint design in this early code were not the same as those for allowable stresses in the timber itself. Fastener loads were entirely dependent upon the group within which the species came and not upon the grade within the species. However, in BS 5268 the strength classes for general stress levels within the timber and for fastener loads are the same, so that there is the presumption that grade within the species does have an effect upon joint capacity. It will presumably be possible to relate most softwood species used in the original structure, and certainly those specified for repair, to the strength classes in the code. For oak values for strength, class D30 should be used.

Bolts

Tables within the code provide allowable loads on bolts for the full range of bolt diameters that the conservator is likely to use. Although they only deal with timber up to 147 mm thick, while some historic timbers are much larger than this, this is not a problem because the allowable loads remain constant beyond a certain thickness. This is because bending of the bolt then becomes the determining factor. (It is worth noting that the 2002 edition of BS 5268 now provides loads for a wider range of bolt sizes and timber thicknesses than the 1996 edition. It is quite possible that the conservator will need to use M10 or M12 bolts in timbers above 50 mm thick.) For softwoods the allowable loads perpendicular to the grain are lower than those parallel to the grain, but the same is not true of oak, where the values are the same.

It has been known for contractors to want to use threaded bar with nuts put on both ends instead of bolts because the bar can be simply cut to the length required. This is not satisfactory because there will be some slippage of the joint as the load is applied and the threads embed themselves into the timber. Also, the bending strength of the stud is significantly lower than that of the bolt. Threaded bar can be used where the fastener is to act in tension.

Coach screws (lag bolts)

One of the most useful fasteners for repair is the hexagonally headed screw. This is because they are inserted and are visible from only one face. Normally referred to as coach screws in Britain, these are called lag bolts in the USA and both terms will be used here depending upon the source referred to. These are not covered by the present BS 5268 and we may first look to American experience for guidance on their use. In some respects, notably their load-carrying capacity, they behave like screws, but in other respects they need to be treated as bolts. Like bolts they are used with a washer under the head and they require a larger pilot hole than ordinary screws. *Wood Handbook* recommends that 'The lead hole for the shank should be the same diameter as the shank. The lead hole for the threaded part varies with the density of the wood'. For denser softwoods, which are those likely to be found for structural use in historic buildings, it recommends a pilot hole for the screw 60–75% of the shank diameter and for hardwoods that it should be 65–85% of the shank diameter. *Wood Handbook* further recommends the use of lubricants for inserting the screws and slightly larger lead holes for longer screws. For some purposes these screws are used in withdrawal where either washers are used under the head or where a steel plate might be necessary.

Experimental work carried out in the USA showed the load capacity of screws in both withdrawal and shear to be a function of the density of the timber. For both ordinary screws and lag bolts the lateral load that could be carried was shown to be given by $F = Kd^2$, where K is dependent upon the density of the timber. These values assumed the screw length in the foundation timber to be 7.5 diameters, with the shank length in the attached timber to be half of that, and the formula applied to both ordinary screws and lag bolts. The values given for ordinary screws in the 1984 edition of BS 5268 used this formula and the values for K were given by Baird and Ozelton (1984) – although they could of course be worked out from the tabulated values of load. Baird and Ozelton noted that no information was provided for coach screws, but suggested the use of the same formula. One difficulty with this (not pointed out by Baird and Ozelton) is that while ordinary screws have the same allowable load irrespective of the direction of loading, the same is not true of lag bolts, for which *Wood Handbook* notes that there is a reduction in load-carrying capacity when loaded perpendicular to the grain. This book provides a table of reduction coefficients for different sizes of bolt.

The figures given in the 1996 code for allowable screw loads threw the general formula into confusion because longer screw lengths were used for most diameters. No figures were given for screws above 8 mm and the formula provided was limited to this size. The position has now improved, with figures tabulated for screws up to 10 mm diameter and with the headside and pointside lengths returned to the earlier values. Only one set of figures are provided, so that the assumption remains that allowable loads on ordinary screws are independent of the direction of loading. This is not an acceptable assumption for coach screws used in softwood, where for bolts there are smaller allowable loads perpendicular to the grain. Therefore it seems prudent to apply the same reduction factor to both coach screws and bolts. In the absence of any other guidance the author has assumed that the formulae given apply only to loads parallel to the grain and has applied a reduction factor for load perpendicular to the grain. This has been derived by taking the ratio of allowable loads on bolts of the same diameter in timbers of thickness 3.5 × the screw diameter. This is a little more generous that the reduction factors suggested in *Wood Handbook*.

The distance of both bolts and coach screws from the edge or end of the timber must also be controlled to prevent splitting of the timber – as must the spacing of these fasteners. These distances depend upon the diameter of the fastener and the direction of the load relative to the edge considered and the direction of grain. These are summarised in Figure 7.2. Screws above 8 mm diameter are treated as if they were bolts for determining spacings in groups of fasteners and for end and edge distances, these being smaller than those required for ordinary screws. This is not explicitly stated in BS 5268, but is the recommendation of the *Timber Construction Manual* (American Institute of Timber Construction, 1985), which states that 'Spacing, end distance, and edge distance requirements for lag bolts are the same as those for bolts of a diameter equal to the shank diameter of the lag bolt' (p. 6-465). The same recommendation is given in STEP 1. This is clearly justified by the larger pilot holes used for coach screws. The same recommendation on coach screw spacing is given in STEP 1, but we should note that the allowable loads for bolts are reduced for spacings of less than 7 diameters. It seems reasonable that the same reduction should be applied to closely spaced coach screws.

Based on this assumption, Table 7.1 provides loads for coach screws between 8 mm and 12 mm in both oak and in C24 softwood,

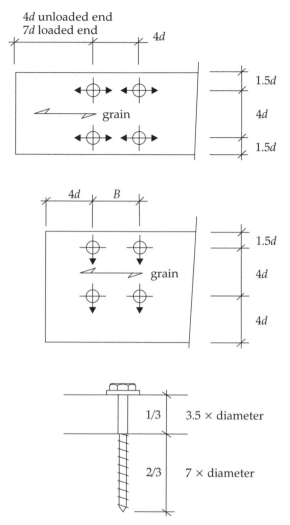

Figure 7.2 Spacing, and edge and end distances of bolts or large diameter coach screws and standard penetration of coach screws.

If $t/d = 1$, $B \geq 3d$
If $t/d \geq 3$, $B \geq 5$
If $1 < t/d < 5$, $B = (2 + d/t)d$

where t = timber thickness, d = bolt diameter

both perpendicular and parallel to the grain. For all other angles Hankinson's formula should be applied (see Appendix 4). The explanation for the difference between oak and softwood is that a principal factor affecting the load that either a bolt or screw will carry is the

Screw diameter	8 mm	10 mm	12 mm
Oak	1398	1727	2463
C24 parallel to grain	1051	1316	1855
C24 perpendicular to grain	967	1145	1614

Table 7.1 Allowable loads in newtons for closely spaced coach screws.

embedding strength. In softwood this is lower when the material is loaded perpendicular to the grain, but in oak is very similar whatever the direction of loading. When the spacing is 7 diameters and above the loads in Table 7.1 may be multiplied by 1.32.

It is important to control the workmanship in making joints with these fasteners. Load-carrying depends upon the minimum head and point lengths being achieved. The screw must not be countersunk into the timber to a depth that would compromise the former and must be long enough to achieve the latter. Any reduction in these two distances results in a corresponding reduction in the allowable load.

Split ring and shear plate connectors

These are used in association with bolts and the groves for the ring or plate are cut with a special cutter once the bolt hole has been drilled. They are normally thought of as being used in the workshop, where the groves can be cut on a bench-mounted drill. However, with care it is possible for them to be cut on site. While split ring connectors are normally used in association with bolts they may also be used with coach screws.

The capacity of split ring connectors may be compared with coach screws. While the former will carry a higher load than a coach screw the spacing of the latter is much smaller. Consider for example the load on a split ring connector in hardwood. The maximum load given in the tables for a 64 mm split ring connector, loaded at parallel to the grain is 13.1 kN, or 24.5 kN for a 102 mm diameter split ring. (The load depends upon the thickness of the timber, but these values are the maximum in each case.) The load on a 12 mm coach screw in the same direction is, from Table 7.1, 2.46 kN. The minimum spacing of the coach screws is 4 diameters in the direction of loading, or 48 mm. In other words it would be possible to place four screws within the area of the smaller split ring to carry a very similar load. The above figures also assume standard end distances, so that the designer needs to make a careful assessment of the likely advantage of using split ring connectors.

Shear plate connectors that are used in association with bolts and steel plates carry a larger load than a split ring of the same size, but have the same requirements for end and edge distances.

Screws in tension

In the design of some joints, such as scarf joints carrying moments, screws act in tension to hold the two pieces of timber together. Thus we are relying upon the purchase of the screw in one piece of timber and the compression under the head of the screw, and its associated washer, in the other. The withdrawal load of the screw is expressed in terms of the load per mm of penetration of the screw into the timber and is dependent upon the diameter of the screw and the density of timber. Again the code provides no figures for coach screws and we must rely on the formulae to derive allowable loads. American tests show that the results for lag bolts are very similar to ordinary screws and the same formula can be applied for both. These results show that the load is directly proportional to the diameter and the depth of penetration of the screw.

For C24 the formula is $P = 3.67d$ N/mm, while for oak $P = 8.43d$ N/mm, where d is the diameter in mm.

The withdrawal load that can be applied to the screw is also limited by the area under the washer. If a standard washer is used that is 3 times the diameter of the screw shank then the allowable load can be assessed by multiplying the bearing area by the allowable stress in compression perpendicular to the grain. In practice, one might assume a slightly higher load because the timber here could be regarded much as a short bearing (see BS 5268 clause 2.10.2), but there has been no experimental work to verify this.

Moisture content and fasteners

The basic load on bolted joints applies to timbers used at an average moisture content below 20%. For timbers that have a moisture content above this a reduction factor of 0.7 should be applied to the basic load to allow for the weakness of green timber. (This factor is applied to the allowable loads for all fasteners.) If a bolted joint is made while the timber has a moisture content above 20%, but which then dries to an average moisture content below this figure in service, a reduction factor of 0.4 should be applied. This is a substantial reduction, to be avoided if possible, and one can see that it is greatly to the advantage of the structural design to be able to obtain dry timber. The logic of this reduction factor is that the shrinkage reduces the size of any hole drilled in the timber as well as its overall dimensions. While the size of the hole will reduce, that of the bolt or coach screw within it will not, resulting in outward forces on the circumference of the hole and possible splitting of the timber (Clauses 6.6.6 – *Permissible load for a joint* and 1.6.4 – *Service classes*). Of course there is the complication in repairs that one half of the fastener will be in green timber and the other half in dry timber.

Although this rule only applies to bolts, with no figure given for screws used in the same circumstances, it is prudent to treat coach screws as if they were bolts for this purpose, especially as it is often the plain shank of the screw that will be in the green, i.e. repair, timber. In the absence of any firm guidance in the code of practice on this matter it would seem sensible simply to allow for the shrinkage in making the hole, i.e. to drill the hole for the bolt or coach screw slightly oversize. With a shrinkage of 5% from green to dry this means a maximum of 0.5 mm for a 10 mm fastener. This is contrary to the normal recommendation for fasteners in dry timber, where the hole diameter should be as close as possible to that of the fastener.

Groups of fasteners in joints

In some cases large moments may have to be transferred from one timber to another, larger than is possible with a single pair of fasteners. For example, Figure 7.3 shows a drawing of a joint required in a main cross beam of a timber frame where the end of the repair had to carry a main post because of the small quantity of original material remaining at this point. However, this load had eventually to be transmitted into the original timber and carried as a bending moment with several fasteners involved in the joint. If it had been a steel connection one would have been happy to carry out an elastic analysis of the joint, distributing the fastener forces accordingly. However, with the extent of movement associated with timber fasteners at high levels of load one can hardly expect a timber joint to behave in a conveniently elastic way. In the event it was assumed that all fasteners would be loaded to their maximum for calculating the resistance of the joint.

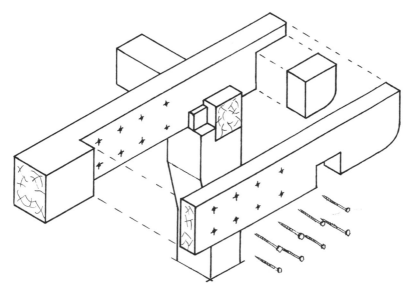

Figure 7.3 A repair with a group of fasteners transmitting a moment from the repair timber into the original timber of the transverse beam of a timber frame.

Timber replacements

A patch at a mortice

This is a fairly common repair in plates or rails as a result of water becoming trapped within the joint or as a result of weathering of the surface. The problem is often exacerbated by unsuitable materials being used for the infill between the studs, and 20th century repair work has often used cement renders on the outer walls, resulting in more water finding its way into these joints. Naturally the repair may involve replacement of the end of the stud or a patch in the timber containing the mortice where a stud tenons into a horizontal member. The function of the joint is to transmit compressive forces across the shoulders of both the tenon and the mortice. If, as is not uncommon, the outer surface has weathered while the inner surface remains sound, a patch will only be required for the external timber (Figure 7.4) fixed with adhesive or with pelleted screws.

Recent work carried out at the Weald and Downland Museum has involved letting replacement timber into the original and fastening it in place with epoxy resin adhesive. The intention is to preserve as much of the original surface as possible so that this remains as a thin 'veneer' over the patch. This has been possible because the structures have been

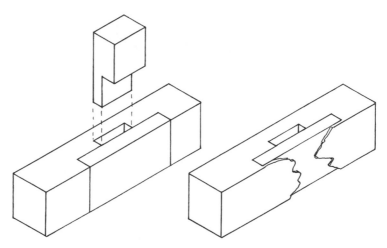

Figure 7.4 Surface patch at mortice and tenon and an alternative repair in which timber is let in behind the original surface thus preserving as much of it as possible. In the first case the repair can be fixed with mechanical fasteners, in the second case with epoxy resin adhesive.

dismantled and the repair made in the workshop. Whether there will be circumstances in which this technique can be adapted to *in situ* repair work remains to be seen. Nevertheless, there are similar structural considerations.

In ideal circumstances the load in the stud will be transmitted evenly across the shoulders of the joint but we cannot assume this to be so. A bare-faced tenon, as shown in Figure 7.4, will bear on one side of the mortice only, but this might also be true of a normal tenon and is especially likely after repair. The fresh surface of the repair timber on one side and the historic timber on the other may well favour the former in transmitting the load and replacement of the tenon itself will make this even more likely. Therefore the fasteners between the repair and the original material should be designed to carry the full load.

Refacing of a member in bending

Two circumstances are possible: loading in the plane of the repair joint and loading at right angles to it.

An example of the former is a repair to the face of a post that is loaded by a brace tenoned into its side (Figure 7.5). The repair made in this situation is similar to the condition described above. It might be possible for either the original timber or the repair timber to carry the bending

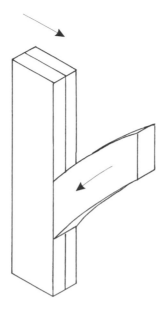

Figure 7.5 Braces loading refaced posts in bending with the brace in the same plane as the repair joint.

moments alone, but it is clearly preferable that they act together. This can be ensured by making sure that load at the mortice is distributed into both members and/or by providing adequate fastenings between the two to ensure that they both deflect together.

Examples of the latter are the refacing of a main post that is loaded by the brace of the cross frame (Figure 7.6) or replacing the soffit of a beam. In the former case the bending moments might be low enough that the sum of the bending resistances of the two timbers acting separately will be sufficient. However, if the two timbers are required to act together then fasteners must be provided to transmit shear across the joint between them. The calculation to determine the force to be transmitted is provided below, but a commonly occurring situation will be where the repair timber is half the depth of the member and this can be treated as a special case.

If we consider this special case and make the distance between the fasteners equal to the depth of the beam, then the shear force at each fastener will be $1.5Q$, where Q is the shear force. While it is possible for fasteners to transfer shear stresses in this way it is normally not possible to transfer the tension forces that result from bending in the member. Therefore, where the repair timber is essential to the bending resistance, it should extend the full length of the member.

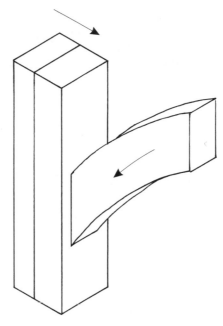

Figure 7.6 Braces loading refaced posts in bending with the brace at right angles to the plane of the repair joint.

The shear stress across the face between the two timbers is a function of the shear force perpendicular to the member and the member geometry. The general expression for this is:

Shear stress $= QAy/Ib$

where Q is the shear force on the section, A is the area above the shear plane, y is the distance of the centroid of this area from the shear plane, I is the second moment of area of the whole cross-section of the beam and b is the width of the shear plane.

For the special case considered where the repair is half of the cross-section:

$A = bd/2, \ y = d/4, \ I = bd^3/12$

Substituting these in the equation above we obtain the result that:

Shear stress $= 1.5Q/bd$

New beam ends

This is such a common circumstance that it needs discussing in some detail. Typical situations are the replacement of the ends of floor joists and beams, roof rafters and tie beams, and repairs to wall plates. Common ways of doing this are to have a scarf or bridle joint between two timbers, to fasten steel plates to the side of the original timber where the decayed material has been replaced or to have a steel flitch within the two timbers. If mechanical fasteners are used a similar calculation is used for all these methods to determine the forces on the joint. If the member is simply in bending then the forces at either end of the joint will be the same, being the moment in the member divided by the length of the joint. This situation can occur in a tie beam where the principal rafter is not directly above the wall plate, thus producing bending in the beam. This assumes there is no other load on the tie beam except its own weight, which might possibly be ignored. Then between the principal rafters the tie will have the tension force combined with a bending moment and there will be no shear force to be considered. However, most members, such as rafters and floor joists, carry a uniformly distributed load (UDL), while wall plates that have a series of rafter loads on them can be treated similarly, i.e. as if the rafters produced a uniformly distributed load. In these members a repair joint has to transmit both a shear force and a bending moment, which means that the forces at each end of the joint will not be the same.

There are two possible arrangements:

(1) The UDL on the member is carried by the original timber across the length of the joint.
(2) The UDL is carried by the repair material across the length of the joint.

Figure 7.7 shows a rather unlikely situation with a member repaired at both ends, but this has been drawn to show both the above configurations. The left-hand end is arrangement 1 while the right-hand end in which the load falls on the new timber for the full length of the joint is arrangement 2. Forces are found by drawing the free body diagram for each repair as shown. The force at the end of the repair is known because this is simply the support reaction for the member, $wl/2$. The load along the member is known, and there are two unknown forces at either end of the joint. These unknown forces can therefore be found by first taking moments about one of them. Having to transmit shear forces as well as bending moments the forces are larger nearer to the supports, i.e. Q is always larger than P. In setting up the equations below it has been assumed that the actual length of the repair is the

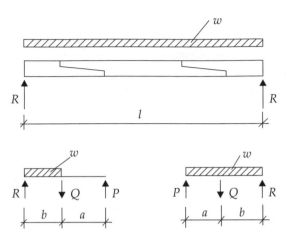

Figure 7.7 Scarf joints in member with UDL with two possible arrangements of loading across the joint.

Refer to Figure 7.7. Assuming a load intensity w/unit length and a span *l* then the load on the member = w*l* and the reaction at each end = w*l*/2.

Let the effective length over which the repair is made be *a*, i.e. the length between the fasteners. This will be a little less than the actual length of the repair because of the addition of end and/or edge distances.

Let the effective additional length to the end of the beam be *b*, i.e the distance between the end fastener or fastener group and the support point of the member.

If the loads on the fasteners are *P* and *Q*:

For condition 1 above:

$$Pa + wb^2/2 - Rb = 0$$

As R is known P can first be found from this equation, when Q is found from:

$$Q + wb = R + P$$

For condition 2 above:

$$R(a+b) - w(a+b)^2/2 - Qa = 0$$

As R is known Q can first be found from this equation, when P is found from:

$$Q + w(a+b) = R + P$$

same as the effective length, i.e. the distance between the fasteners, or groups of fasteners, although this introduces a slight error.

While this has been shown for a scarf joint, the equations will also apply to other repairs, such as steel plates fastened by bolts or screws as in Figure 7.14.

The methods of repair are described below.

Tabled scarf joint

This is a popular repair because the result is visually pleasing. The joint can be used where the repair is to be seen and is therefore one of the most common forms of repair in timber-framed buildings (Figure 7.8). In making the repair the cut in the original timber is made first and the new timber fitted to this. Tightness can be ensured in the joint by setting up the joint and running a saw kerf along the squint at both ends so that sliding the timber up makes both squints tight. Clearly, if this method is used, for the joint to fit properly the timber of the repair has to be a little deeper than the original and must then be brought to a fit by planing once the joint has been completed. If the screws or bolts are simply set orthogonal to the member, as they are tightened up, they will produce a component of force along the plane of the table tending to drive the two timbers apart. Therefore it is better to have them perpendicular to the plane of the table. Of course this will be essential if split ring connectors are to be used in the joint.

It is worth considering the design of these scarf joints under bending loads because of their popularity. Their behaviour is not well understood, but TRADA has carried out tests on such joints assembled using a number of different fasteners in order to ascertain their relative strength and their strength compared with the parent timber. These tests suggest that their limiting moment capacity is equal to $\frac{1}{3}$ of the moment capacity of the parent timber, so it would be prudent to limit the moment on any repair joint to this value. However, this does not help when there is also shear on the joint, and we may consider a simple model as a means of assessing the forces for the purposes of design.

For simplicity consider a joint in pure bending – as in Figure 7.8. In a simple, bolted side-by-side scarf (and in a bridle joint – see below) there are simply shear forces in the bolts holding the timbers together. However, in a tabled scarf joint the force at one end is provided by tension in the fastener (possibly a coach screw), while at the other end there will be direct compression between the timbers over an unknown length. The area in compression might be found by dividing the force at the end of

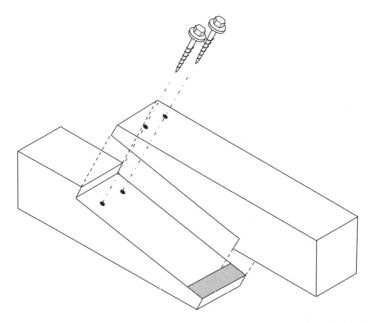

Figure 7.8 Tabled scarf joint using coach screws in withdrawal. The shaded area shows the area that will be in compression as moment comes onto the joint.

the joint by the allowable compression stress perpendicular to the grain. The distance from the centre of this compression area to the fasteners at the other end is therefore the effective length of the joint.‡ In practice, members will normally be transmitting a shear force as well as bending so that the forces at either end of the joint will not be the same. However, the principle for determining effective length is the same.

Design of the joint involves balancing the length of the scarf with the load the fasteners are required to carry. Carpenters normally make the length of the scarf 2½ to 3 times the depth of the timber. There will usually be sufficient depth to use a screw, which will be loaded in withdrawal. There are no recommendations for the end distance to be used for either screws or bolts under this kind of loading, but the author commonly uses 4 diameters or the depth of timber under the head of the screw if larger.

Structural considerations suggest that the tension side of the joint should be placed further from the support, because it will then have the smaller load on it. However, this may not be the most desirable from visual considerations. Where a member is visible one would, given a

---

‡ Some engineers might prefer to take a triangular distribution of stress, but this seems unduly cautious.

choice, want to show less of the repair timber, leaving more of the original in view. In a wall plate repair to an open roof more original timber is left visible if the tension end of the joint is furthest from the support because the new timber will be on the outside. However, the reverse is true of repairs to joist or beam ends visible from below where the new timber needs to be on the upper surface. The same is true of rafters in open roofs, where it is also desirable that as little new wood as possible be exposed. These are examples where visual considerations can override structural ones.

Scarf with side load

The repair above considers a joint in bending as in Figure 7.9(a), in which coach screws are used in withdrawal. However, the same basic

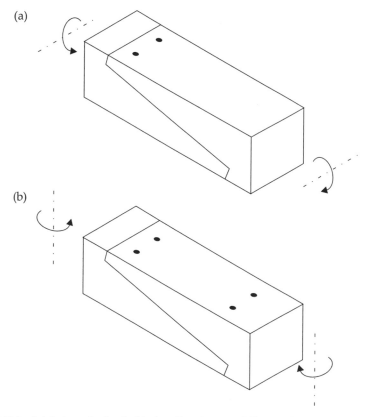

Figure 7.9 A joint can be loaded in bending in two different directions. Joists and rafters are likely to be repaired as (a) but wall plates might well be repaired as (b) with the fasteners acting in shear.

carpentry might be used in the repair of a wall plate where bending is in the other direction, as in Figure 7.9(b), and the joint is fastened together with two pairs of bolts or screws acting in shear. Here the load characteristics of the fasteners and the practicalities of construction are rather different. The allowable load on the bolt depends upon the thickness of timber through which it passes and it is clearly desirable to ensure that both ends of the bolt are within the same thickness of timber. While the nut end may be countersunk and pelleted into the deeper side of the scarf, one could use domed headed coach bolts on the thinner side, which may be visually acceptable. Thus for bolts the nut side of the scarf should ideally only be thicker than the head side by the thickness required for sinking the nut. For screws the angle of the table might be determined by the greater depth of timber required for the point side of a screw.

Halved scarf joint

The half scarf joint (Figure 7.10) is structurally the simplest method of joining two pieces of timber to transmit shear and bending. It was the form of scarf joint adopted in the 19th century as a means of forming

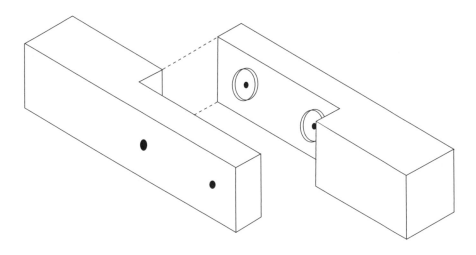

Figure 7.10 Scarf joint with split ring connectors. This joint will be loaded as in Figure 7.9(a).

long tie beams from more than one timber with bolts in shear transmitting the tension force. When this form of joint is used to transmit moments it might be convenient to use split ring connectors or shear plates. The cross-section is halved, so the moment that can be transmitted across the joint will only be half of the capacity of the full size beam.

Bridle joint

The advantage of the bridle joint (Figure 7.11) is that it involves the least loss of original timber. If the decayed end of the member is cut off, the only other loss is the material required for the slot into which the tenon on the replacement timber is fixed. The tenon will then normally be fixed by a bolt though the timbers. The load-carrying capacity will be limited either by the bending capacity of the tenon or by the capacity of the bolts. If a single fastener is used at each end the design of these joints will be largely governed by the loaded edge distance on the bolts, especially in small members such as roof rafters. The sensible way to cut

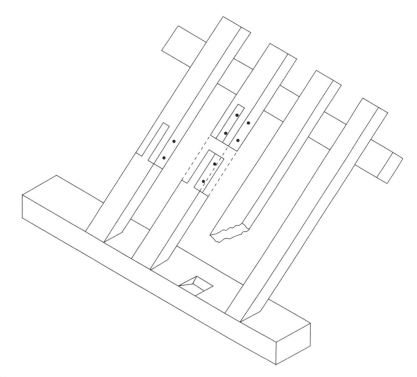

Figure 7.11 Bridle joints used to repair decayed rafter ends.

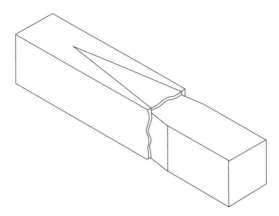

Figure 7.12 V joint suitable for end replacement using epoxy resin adhesive.

the joint is to make the tenon one third of the width of the original timber, so this limits the bending capacity of the joint to one third that of the original.

V joints

A joint devised by the Weald and Downland Museum might be regarded as a modern version of the bridle joint. A V-shaped cut is made in the beam and a corresponding timber let into this and fastened with epoxy resin (Figure 7.12). As with their mortice repair, the purpose is to retain as much of the original timber surface as possible. This also has the advantage over the bridle joint that no mechanical fasteners are used, so that it is more 'discrete'.

Scissor scarfs

This complex version of the scarf joint has been used to replace the decayed ends of posts (Figure 7.13). They have to transmit not only the compression load in the post but also moments induced by wind loading or even accidental loading of the post itself. Their advantage is that they will transmit bending moments in either direction without the aid of fasteners. As a moment is applied the ends go into compression on either side of the joint. It is not clear what stresses are developed within the joint itself. There is also a practical difficulty in making the joint *in situ*, because clearance as long as the joint is required below the base of the post.

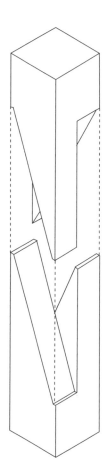

Figure 7.13 Scissor scarf.

Butt joints with steel plates

These have the advantage that the least amount of original timber is removed and they are very simple to make as *in situ* repairs for rehabilitation work, requiring little carpentry skill. There are two ways of handling this type of repair: either to use a flitch plate between the two timbers or to use plates either side. The latter is not usually suitable where the repair is visible. Load transfer is from timber to plate and then from plate back to timber, but it may be possible, and indeed easier, to rely upon the steel alone to transfer load from the sound part of the beam to the support. In these circumstances the decayed timber might be replaced simply to prevent buckling of the steel plates and/or to transfer load from floor or ceiling joists (Figure 7.14). Some provision

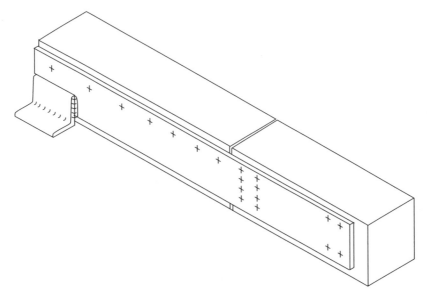

Figure 7.14 Beam end replacement with steel plates. A timber packing is screwed between the steel plates to prevent their buckling and angles have been welded to the ends to provide adequate bearing.

will then have to be made for bearing at the ends of the steel plates, for example by bolting or welding steel angles to their ends. Design of the repair involves balancing the length of the repair plate against the number of fasteners required.

Flitch plates and reinforcing bars

When flitch plates are used for this kind of repair they are often fastened to the timber with an epoxy resin adhesive. This avoids the problem of drilling and lining up bolt holes in the plate and the timber. It is not usual to carry out calculations of the bond between the epoxy resin and the other materials because experience shows that it is the strength of the timber that governs the design. The alternative to steel plates is reinforcing bars set in epoxy resin, and work has been done on the design of these. Jones and Smedley (2000) report that when using steel reinforcing bars with epoxy, joint efficiencies depend upon the size of the original timber, varying from 63% for 150 × 50 beams to 97% for 175 × 50. The purpose of the repair is to replace decayed beam ends so that they would be used in regions of low bending moment but relatively high shear. The results show that where joints were in the region

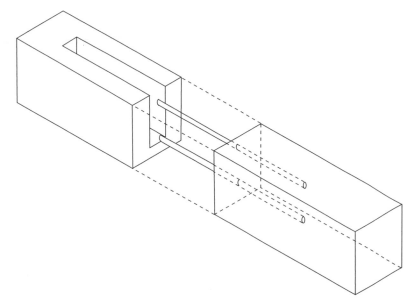

Figure 7.15 Beam end replacement using epoxy resin and reinforcing bars to join the new timber end to the existing timber.

of high shear stress, failure still occurred in the bending section of the beam. In other words the joint carried all the shear that was required. The joint is made by fixing reinforcing bars into the replacement end and making a slot in the end of the original beam (Figure 7.15). The replacement timber can then be placed into position with the projecting bars let into the slot. The repair is completed by pouring an epoxy mortar into the slot and round the reinforcing bars. The method of design that they suggest is similar to that used for reinforced concrete beams, in which the timber carries compressive stresses only. It should be noted that a difficulty with epoxy resin is controlling the flow of the material and preventing it from getting onto the surfaces, where it can be at best unsightly and may do irreparable damage to historic finishes.

Strengthening members in bending

Both flitch plates and reinforcing rods are also used for improving the bending strength (or stiffness) of beams. The most obvious need for this is when rehabilitation of a building involves floor loads that are higher than the existing structure is able to carry safely. In these circumstances some strengthening of primary beams may be necessary. However, similar repairs might be required if there is a defect at, or close to, the mid-span of a beam. There have even been cases where the depth of a beam has been reduced by the removal of timber in an attempt to produce a level soffit after the beam has deflected. There is little choice in these cases except to reinforce the beam in some way. If the beam is completely concealed then a wide range of approaches might be possible, including the simple addition of steel plates or trussing on the side of the beam. If access to the top of the beam is possible then steel flitches or reinforcing can be let into a chainsaw cut, and this type of repair can be used for structures where the beam is partly exposed. Where access to the top of the beam is impossible the use of carbon fibre reinforcing strips let into the sides of the beam might be used. However, this last approach, which requires the use of epoxy resin adhesives, must be regarded as a specialist job and will not be dealt with here.

Both flitch plates and steel plates bolted to the sides of a timber to increase its load-carrying capacity involve the same calculations for determining the sizes required. The strength of the steel flitch cannot simply be added to that of the beam because of the differences in their elastic properties. Steel has a very much higher modulus of elasticity than timber, so that for any given deflection of the flitch beam the stress in the steel will be very much higher than the stress in the timber. How much higher can be seen simply by comparing their moduli of elasticity. The modulus of elasticity of steel is 205×10^3 N/mm^2, whereas the minimum value for THA oak (the value to be used for a beam) is about 10×10^3 N/mm^2. The stress in the steel will be a little more than 20 times the stress in the oak for the same deflection. More significantly, we can compare the relative allowable working stresses. That for steel is 180 N/mm^2, and dividing by 20.5 gives 8.8 N/mm^2, which is below the maximum allowable stress for this timber. Thus when the steel has reached its maximum stress the stress in the timber will be below the maximum allowed, so it will no longer be carrying the load that it did before the flitch was added. The way to design a flitch beam is to consider deflections, because as the beam bends the deflection of both the timber and steel must be the same. The question to be resolved is the distribution of the load between them.

The deflection of a beam under uniformly distributed loading is given by $\delta = 5WL^3/384EI$.

If a steel beam and a timber beam each have a load applied to them, $\delta_s = 5 W_s L^3/384E_s I_s$ and $\delta_t = 5W_t L^3/384E_t I_t$, where W_s and W_t are the

Flitch plate

Softwood

E (timber) @	7.2×10^6		f_t @	7.5 N/mm^2
E (steel) @	205×10^6		f_s @	180
Original beam – width @	200 mm		depth @	300 mm
$z =$	3×10^6 mm^3			
Allowable BM =	22.5 kN m			
Required BM @	40 kN m			
Let b_s be	10 mm		then $b_t =$	190 mm
$BM_s =$	23.99 kN m		$BM_t =$	16.01 kN m
$z_s =$	0.15		$z_t =$	2.87
$f_s =$	160 N/mm^2		$f_s =$	5.62 N/mm^2

Oak

E (timber) @	10.5×10^6		f_t @	12.6 N/mm^2
E (steel) @	205×10^6		f_s @	180
Original beam – width @	200 mm		depth @	300 mm
$z =$	3×10^6 mm^3			
Allowable BM =	37.8 kN m			
Required BM @	50 kN m			
Let b_s be	10 mm		then $b_t =$	190 mm
$BM_s =$	25.34 kN m		$BM_t =$	24.66 kN m
$z_s =$	0.15		$z_t =$	2.85
$f_s =$	177 N/mm^2		$f_s =$	8.65 N/mm^2

loads carried and δ_s and δ_t are the deflections of the steel and timber respectively.

As $\delta_s = \delta_t$ and therefore $5W_s L^3/384E_s I_s = 5W_t L^3/384E_t I_t$, if the span is the same, $W_s/E_s I_s = W_t/E_t I_t$.

$I = bd^3/12$, and if we assume that the flitch will be the same depth as the parent beam, this reduces to $W_t/E_t b_t = W_s/E_s b_s$, where b is the width of the material. This provides the distribution of the loads between the two materials for a given applied load. Of course the total load carried by the beam is $W = W_s + W_t$, so that we can substitute either of the above to find the load carried by the steel or the timber, for example $W_s = W/(1 + E_t b_t/E_s b_s)$.

How this works in practice can be seen from the practical examples with both softwood and oak beams. In these calculations the loads on the beams have been replaced by the bending moments they are required to carry. A 10 mm plate has been used with the result that the plate carries more than half of the required moment and the stresses in both materials are well below the maximum allowed. With the oak beam the steel stress is closer to the maximum allowed, but it still carries almost half the applied moment. Of course, the slot cut for the steel (and hence the steel itself) will usually be slightly shallower than the original beam and the simplification used above will not apply.

It is not always possible to bolt the steel to the timber because of problems of access. If the timber is exposed this might also be regarded as unsightly. These are sometimes the reasons why epoxy resin is used to bond the steel plate to the timber. A satisfactory repair can often more easily be made using a T-section steel let into a slot, as with a steel plate, but fastened down to the top of the beam with coach screws. In practice the T-section will normally be formed of two angle sections back to back. Assume in the example above that we are looking for steels to carry the whole of the bending moment, i.e. two angles are required to carry 15 kN m each. Using standard steel tables this is provided by 2 no. 100 × 65 mm steel angles. It is apparent that this can be a more convenient method of strengthening the beam because it requires the cutting of a much shallower slot.

Provision of supplementary structure

Complete supplementary structure

This is the kind of work that requires an experienced engineer, and the situations that are likely to be encountered are too varied to make a detailed discussion here particularly useful. An example of a structure of this type was provided for a building in Marktheidenfeld, Franconia which had been formed in the 18th century from two adjacent medieval buildings. In doing this a large upper floor room was created that was partly in each of the two original buildings. The result was a loss of integrity of the roof supports. To preserve the 18th century room intact and provide a satisfactory roof structure a steel structure had to be inserted in the roof. This was done while preserving the roof timbers as found and still using the original rafters to support the roof covering.

As the carpenter or architect may well become involved in the discussion of the design of such work, it is worth briefly noting the issues that might be raised. The first is of course the loads that are to be carried by the new structure. In this type of reinforcement there is no attempt to maintain the behaviour of the original structure. Even if it is possible to do so, such an approach would involve an unacceptable loss of historic fabric or historic character. Therefore the original structure will remain as simply a secondary structure transferring loads to the new primary structure that is to be inserted. Based on this assumption, the loads to the new primary structure can be determined. The new structure will, of course, have to be built with minimal disruption of the historic fabric, and this must be a primary concern in its design. The engineer will need to consider the method of construction and discuss this with other members of the design team.

Much more common is the insertion of a supplementary structure designed to act in concert with the original. Examples here are the insertion of bracing to prevent racking in tall roofs, the insertion of wind bracing to cope with transverse wind loads that are inadequately catered for by the original structure, and the strengthening of roofs with inadequate purlins or wall plates. In all these examples the need for remedial work will be apparent through deformations in the structure which, while not yet fatal, might result in severe damage or even collapse if left unchecked. This may eventually be caused by secondary forces arising as a result of the deformations or because of weakening of the structure through decay and eventual damage in an exceptional storm – or possibly a combination of these.

A fairly commonly occurring situation involves inadequate purlins or wall plates in barns. In some 18th century barns where softwood was used in place of oak this was done with no corresponding increase in member sizes. One sometimes finds structures with excessively long bays, possibly in an attempt to economise on timber, or structures where the original covering has been replaced with something heavier. Wall plates as well as purlins may be too small in barns with timber-framed walls, where the weight of the roof is carried by the wall studs but where the magnitude of the outward thrust has not been recognised. Although, when originally built, the stresses in these members may have exceeded those that would be allowed by modern codes, the only signs of distress would have been large deflections. But these will have increased over the years as a result of creep, and with time and decay the structure may now be in a critical condition. Of course, this process is accelerated if the deflections are sufficient to compromise the ability of the covering to exclude rain.

In such cases one method of repair is to provide some form of supplementary structure while at the same time possibly bringing the structure back towards its original geometry, so that the roof can be made to work properly. If the latter is required then at least partial removal of the covering will be required. The wall plate and purlins could be stiffened by adding additional timber or by reinforcing with steel plates.

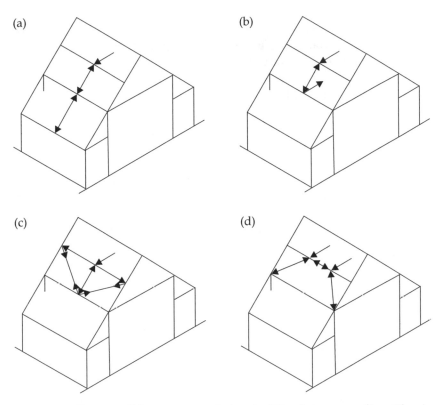

Figure 7.16 Four possible arrangements for strutting between purlins. The simplest are (a) and (b). (c) and (d) could be used if there is insufficient headroom for a tie between the arcade plates or the aisle can provide no resistance.

However, it is also possible to strut and tie the purlin and plates at mid-span, so reducing the bending moments. Schemes for such reinforcing for an aisled barn are shown in Figures 7.16(a)–(c). A commonly seen attempt to remedy weak purlins was to strut between them. However, this can only be effective if there is some vertical force provided as well, or at least some force with a vertical component. The obvious solution is to provide a force in the plane of the rafters, and this can be done by strutting from the arcade plate. This or course imposes an additional horizontal force on the arcade plate, which may already be over-stressed. If the arcade plate itself requires assistance this might be provided by the aisle structure (a) or by simply tying directly across to the other plate (b). If there is insufficient headroom for the latter and the first is not possible then a truss might be created within the roof plane, the compression members of which will be the purlins (Figure 7.16(c)).

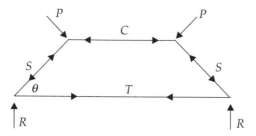

Figure 7.17 Forces in the frame shown in 7.16(a). The force R is a load on the arcade plate.

The fourth possibility with two struts (Figure 7.16(d)) will involve using the arcade plate as a tie.

Consider first the bending moments on the purlins. These beams are divided into two by the additional structure and so will behave as continuous beams over a central support. Comparing the support forces and moments of Figures 7.16(a)–(c), it is clear that the bending moments are now ¼ of the original bending moments, providing an adequate support force of 0.625W can be provided (where W is the UDL on the purlin). Note that with the structure already deflected this force will not be generated unless the members in bending are strained back to their 'original' position. In practice this may not be possible, and only partial recovery from the deflected shape may be achievable. In this case the forces in the supplementary structure will be lower than those to be calculated below and the reduction of bending moment will be less.

The supplementary structure is effectively a tied arch with two point loads on it (Figure 7.17). If the purlin load is P then:

$C = P \sin \theta$

$R = P \cos \theta$ and $R = S \sin \theta$ from which $S = P \cos \theta / \sin \theta$

$T = S \cos \theta$

The supplementary structure shown in Figure 7.16(c) was contemplated for the repair of a medieval barn in which the purlins were inadequate to carry what was almost certainly a heavier roof covering than the original. These purlins had failed, with visible fractures, and the intention was to reduce the purlin stresses. Strutting these with collars and struts to the arcade plates was contemplated with ties back from these plates to the ends of the purlins. In the event it was found possible to add steel angles between the purlins and their seating on the principal rafters and projecting far enough to reduce the effective span

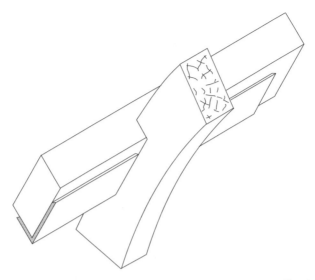

Figure 7.18 Steel supports under a timber purlin reducing its effective span.

of the timbers (Figure 7.18). Because the purlins were continuous over two bays the length of these steel supports could be adjusted to ensure that the points of contraflexure under dead load coincided with the observed fractures in the timbers (Yeomans and Smith, 2000).

Previous repairs

In many cases the conservator will be confronted with a structure that has already been repaired in the past, and such repairs may be considered to have significance as part of the history of the building. They are, of course, indications of the inadequacy of the original design and so provide some insight into the structural knowledge of both the original builders and of those who made the repairs. Some will be adequate repairs that can be left to do their job, some may have proved inadequate or have become inadequate as a result of further changes in the structure and so will require new structure, and some may be little more than inadequate bodges. For all of these situations difficulties may occur if the presence of the earlier repair compromises the design presently being considered. It seems sensible to make a judgement about the value of an historic repair in the same way that one would make a judgement about the value of any other aspect of the historic fabric. This of course means bringing to bear some knowledge of the history of structural design as it applies to this kind of structure, so that the historic significance of the work can be assessed. If the repair is simply an inadequate bodge, and many are, then there seems little point in retaining it if the present work would be better without it.

8

Surveying for repair

The survey stage is perhaps the most important part of the work, because it is here that any structural problems are diagnosed and where possible solutions start to be considered. It is essential to have a full understanding of the condition of the structure before any actions are proposed; in fact before it is decided whether any action is required at all. Although the word 'survey' is used for simplicity, the terms 'structural appraisal' or 'structural assessment' might be more appropriate, because the principal concern is the adequacy of the structure to carry loads rather than a complete survey of the building. The information gathered will be restricted to what is sufficient for that purpose. Nevertheless, it is also important to understand the history of the structure, because deterioration and changes made during its lifetime will have affected its structural behaviour. Explaining the structure's history may well be the most significant part of the work.

The purpose of any survey determines both what is examined and the means by which observations are recorded. A survey must also involve some interpretation, because what one observes will in turn affect what one measures. Finding signs of distress in a structure may, for example, suggest further investigation in order to determine the precise extent of the problem or to search for causes. It is regrettable that too often building surveys are carried out without the advice of an engineer, resulting in very detailed drawings of the fabric that are of little use for the structural appraisal. The engineer's concerns are clearly different from those of the architect, who might be looking at other aspects of the building, and suggests that individual professionals need to do their own surveys. But it may be possible to use drawings made by others as a starting point.

A structural appraisal may be required either as part of the preliminary work in planning rehabilitation work, or because signs of distress have been found in a building. Not uncommonly both occur at the same time, i.e. the rehabilitation work uncovers signs of structural distress. These signs of distress might have been caused by past changes that have now stabilised or might be the result of ongoing action that needs to be addressed. The ultimate purpose therefore is to recommend repairs that have to be made or possibly some strengthening of the building so that it will be fit for its new purpose. Therefore the survey is not a completely separate activity from that of making recommendations for repair. The engineer will have in mind the possible need for calculations to determine the strength of particular elements of the structure and so will be building up a model of the structural actions.

Rehabilitation work might involve alterations to the structure as well as repair, with the structure possibly being asked to carry greater loads than those it has carried in the past; alternatively, some change in the load-carrying mechanism may be required. Thus the intentions of the client will be an important consideration. In historically significant buildings the value of the historic fabric will also act as a constraint upon any recommendations made. It is therefore important that all those working on the structure have some understanding of the historic value of the fabric so that any recommended work will be sensitive to that.

Put simply, the purposes of the survey are:

- To note signs of distress in the structure and any structural damage or deterioration.
- To determine the causes of the above.
- To determine whether or not the observed behaviour has stabilised.
- To determine any urgent measures that need to be carried out.
- To gather sufficient information to enable recommendations to be made for any remedial work that might be necessary.

or

- To determine the present condition of the structure as a preliminary step in the rehabilitation of the building.

The first task is to build up an overall picture of a building's structural behaviour. It is difficult to imagine looking at a structure without doing this, which is perhaps the core skill of the structural engineer. This then guides one in deciding what aspects of the structure need to be looked at in detail. At the same time it is important to note changes within the building that may well have altered its structural behaviour or have led to signs of distress that have been observed. The type of building being surveyed will suggest the basic structural forms that one should expect to see. One should then note the obvious changes that have been made to the building and the sequence of such events. In some cases there might be documentary evidence of the original form of the building. Nevertheless, one always needs to ask whether there are any features that point to obvious changes in the structure.

The ideal situation is where the architect calls one in at the preliminary stage so that the structural survey and recommendations for repair can be part of the design process. Unfortunately it is not uncommon that one is called in because some problem has been discovered during the repair work. This makes the work more difficult and may well increase the costs. What seems to be difficult in this kind of work is to persuade the client that money will be saved by a proper survey at the beginning. One psychological difficulty is that if the job is properly done in this way there will be a period at the beginning where the client will be aware that costs are being incurred but where nothing appears to be happening.

The basic process

The ideal process has been described in the guidelines set out by ISCARSAH.* This uses a medical analogy to describe the process in which a doctor carries out an examination of a patient, diagnoses the problem and recommends some cause of action. This is a useful analogy because many aspects of the doctor's work have parallels in the conservation of a structure. We expect the doctor to have a knowledge of anatomy and of the various diseases that can affect the patient, just as we expect the conservator to understand the construction and behaviour of a building. Doctors are limited in the extent to which they can examine patients and in the recommendations that they can make, and similar constraints apply to the conservator. It is helpful to consider the process in this light.

Anatomy

Understanding the anatomy of buildings requires some elaboration. It means knowing how they were built, what kinds of changes were

---

* The International Scientific Committee for the Analysis and Restoration of Structures of Architectural Heritage (an ICOMOS committee) has recently produced a set of Principles and Guidelines.

common to them and what kinds of 'diseases' they are prone to. For example, 18th century roofs are prone to timber decay because of deteriorating roof lead-work, and bond timbers and beam-ends in walls are similarly vulnerable. These are aspects of their construction that one would be conscious of in surveying such buildings. Such knowledge is also important in being able to separate the commonly occurring phenomena that perhaps have no structural significance from those that are peculiar to the structure under examination and thus are cause for concern. We all know that the roofs of some buildings tend to be rather wavy, and this is because the purlins, loaded while still green, have suffered from creep. This common phenomenon does not mean that a particular roof is about to collapse. That timber frame buildings appear to be tipping forward into the street because of the shrinkage of the timber in the front walls does not mean that they are actually about to fall into the street. Large timbers exhibit drying checks and these may have little structural significance.[†]

In Britain we are fortunate that historic buildings have been thoroughly studied so that we have a good account of their basic anatomy, but this is not always the case. When working in other countries it may be necessary first to try to understand the construction and resulting structural behaviour of the building type before trying to understand the problems of a particular example. Unfortunately, even local professionals may have a poor knowledge of the construction of their own historic buildings because of a lack of tradition of both academic study and restoration of their historic structures – the very reason why one may be asked to work there. The way in which medical students acquire their knowledge of anatomy is through the dissection of cadavers, and this would be an ideal way for engineers to acquire their knowledge of building anatomy, i.e. by looking at buildings in the process of demolition.

Abuses

Human bodies are not just subject to disease; they are also subject to abuse by their owners, and the results of such abuse may occasion a visit to the doctor. Buildings may also exhibit distress both because of what owners have done to them in the past through ill-advised alterations and what they have not done through neglect. It is difficult to

---

† Nevertheless, it is surprising how often consultants for major buildings have, in ignorance, had these checks filled with epoxy resin.

imagine a building of any age or size that has not experienced some change, and changes were often made without any concern for the integrity of the structure. Therefore understanding the anatomy of a particular building means understanding its history – not a matter of dates, although that will have influenced the technologies employed, but principally the sequence of events. While a human patient will have a medical record, so might the history of a building have left some documentary trace, and a desk study of the available information is a useful preliminary to the physical survey of the building.

A possible difficulty is that the client may not understand the necessity for what may appear to be merely an academic exercise. Nevertheless, a proper understanding of the building's history will often avoid unpleasant surprises. Of course, just as buildings of a similar type may be subject to similar problems of decay, so buildings of a similar age have often suffered similar kinds of alteration, and a brief review of the types of buildings discussed here may be useful.

Medieval buildings

The most common alterations to medieval buildings include the insertion of floors and chimneys, alterations of roof profiles, and the cladding of the timber frame with masonry, either totally or in part. As with buildings of any period, changes to the plan do sometimes involve fairly radical alterations to the structure.

Medieval buildings had an open fire in the hall and some kind of smoke hood in the roof, and the evidence of this can often still be seen in smoke-blackened roof timbers. Later, when fireplaces and chimneys were adopted, they were inserted into existing buildings either by being attached to an outside wall or by being placed at the centre of one end of the hall. The former required some interruption of the external wall structure, while the latter might involve cutting into roof trusses and so cutting through roof tie beams. Thus the chimney might become part of the structure of the building, and where tie beams have been cut through it may be necessary to ensure proper connection to the masonry.

The roofs of some buildings often survive intact, even when major changes have been made in the rooms below, including the insertions of floors (and therefore staircases). In others the roof may have been raised in order to increase the volume of accommodation on the upper floor. In such instances only fragments of the original roof will survive, if any. It will be necessary to ensure that the new roof has a properly

supported wall plate and is adequately tied. Another alteration sometimes seen in a roof is the extension of a hip roof to a full gable or
chimney stack in the end wall that involves extending the ridge. It may
then be necessary for remedial work to ensure proper support of the
ridge if this was not provided in the original alteration.

As noted in Chapter 2, the present property divisions may not be
those that existed in the past. Simple extensions to a free-standing
building are sometimes apparent in weathered timber surfaces that are
now within the building. In such cases the integrity of the original
structure might not have been compromised and it is a matter of
ensuring the adequacy of the connection. It is more likely for the integrity of the structure to have been compromised where a building has
been subdivided, or extended into a neighbouring property that has in
consequence been subdivided. In such cases new load paths may have
been created.

The creation of new load paths is most commonly seen at the ground
floor when what were simple dwellings or medieval workshop premises in town centres have been converted to more modern commercial uses: either shops or public houses. The kind of changes commonly
seen are the removal of ground floor wall structures to create shop windows, the opening up of part of the wall to make bay windows or even
the removal of main corner posts to make doorways. Plan changes
might require the removal of the base of crucks to facilitate circulation
at ground floor level, thus requiring the provision of a beam to carry the
structure above. As altered, the building may still have a satisfactory
structure, even though many changes are made without an apprecia-
tion of either the overall structural behaviour or the new load path created. More serious is the removal of braces in box-frame buildings,
which will probably result in some sidesway of the structure and remedial action of some kind to arrest that movement.

Replacement of wattle infill with brick noggin is the most common
change seen in the materials of construction. Apart from the increased
load that this places on the structure, the most serious effect is often to
compromise the weathering performance of the structure and encourage
decay in main structural timbers. The more vulnerable areas are the joints:
either the feet of studs where they tenon into plates and the lower ends of
braces where they meet the posts. Naturally, both timbers are subject to
decay at these points. The problem is made worse if the brickwork has
been rendered over to preserve the black and white effect.

Of course the brickwork provides an alternative load path, so that
any movement of the building following its insertion into the frame is
likely to result in a shift of load from the frame to the brickwork.

Examples have been seen where this has been accompanied by changes in the plan involving the removal of parts of the timber frame, producing, in part, a load-bearing brick masonry structure. Accidental loading of brick infill might occur because of decay of the timber and shedding of load to the brick. If the brick is only a single 4½" (114 mm) leaf this can result in a wall likely to fail in buckling, so that it could be important to restore the original timber frame action.

Replacement of roofing material will involve a change in the weight of the roof, and if the change is from thatch to stone slate the result may be a roof that is rather weak for the load that it is now being called upon to carry. The common result is that the purlins will be inadequate, deflecting so that more load has to be picked up by the rafters.

The practice of adding masonry fronts to existing timber frame buildings as fashions changed may superficially disguise the real nature of the construction. Although earlier examples in stone are found, this was very commonly done in brick in the 18th century, when it is called Georgianising. The practised eye will often be able to spot this in urban buildings from the outside simply by the scale of a building in comparison to its later neighbours. Sometimes only the front of the building was Georgianised, leaving the timber frame exposed on the less publicly visible rear and sides. Examples can also be found where the ground floor has been changed to masonry with a timber structure remaining above. A masonry front may be added in such a way that it either encases the timbers of the original building or replaces them, or it may simply be placed in front of the timbers. This practice was not confined to dwellings, but can also be seen where masonry walls have been added to barns.

Improvements to interior finishes are linked to the fashion change evident in the Georgianising of the front elevation. Interiors were given a plaster finish, and this frequently involved hacking over the surface of the timbers to provide a key for the plaster. More seriously, it might also involve the cutting back of timbers to reduce their size so that they were flush with the rest of the wall, and naturally this can compromise the structure. Sometimes later plaster work has been subsequently removed as fashions changed again, leaving the rough surface of the timber as a tell-tale sign of what has been done. In some instances the original wattle and daub fill of internal partitions may have survived these changes.

Eighteenth century buildings

A large proportion of our building stock comprises buildings of the 18th and 19th centuries, and because many of these are close to town centres they have often been converted from domestic to commercial uses. Although this will have involved less radical changes than those made to medieval buildings, they can nevertheless be structurally significant. Also, buildings in the 18th century were put up at a time of changing structural design. The simple types of roof structure that had come down from the middle ages were being superseded by a radically different type that was not always fully understood by the carpenters that were attempting to build them. This was because their source of knowledge was largely based on copying structures built by others or from drawings in carpenters' books, without fully understanding what it was they were copying. The result can be something that superficially resembles the new structural form but which is poorly proportioned or incorrectly detailed.

As the 18th century house was a timber structure within a brick shell, trussed partitions were used so that walls did not have to carry through from one floor to another. Subsequent plan changes sometimes involved changes in the position of doors and there have been cases where the new doorways have been cut through important structural timbers within these partitions. The result would be excessive deflections as the trussing action was affected and members had to carry loads in bending. This was less likely to occur where the trussing was confined to the area above the door head, although the insertion of a new doorway might still involve cutting through a post carrying load from the plate below. The obvious difficulty here is to know what framing exists behind the plaster of the wall. Simple survey methods might tell one very little, and X-ray or thermal imaging methods might be needed in some circumstances.

Little need be said about floors. Where these have sagged over time joists may have been firred to bring the floor back to level. The most common damage to floors is the cutting of notches for running services, since plumbers and electricians seem to have a disregard of structure. Where notches are close to supports there will be a reduction in shear capacity but this will seldom be serious. It is notches at mid-span or where there is continuity over a supporting wall that present a problem, and in some cases it might be necessary to carry out remedial action to restore the bending resistance of joists or beams. The other possible problem is the decay of beam-ends in walls.

Although not part of the timber structure, any survey of an 18th century building should take account of the likely presence of bond timbers within the masonry. These were included to prevent cracking of the masonry round doors and windows and normally comprise long timber plates set into the inner leaf of brickwork. Naturally these have proved vulnerable to decay, and today are commonly cut out and replaced with reinforced concrete.

The investigation

Armed, one hopes, with some knowledge of the anatomy of the building, the problems that it is subjected to and the kinds of abuses that it might have suffered, the conservator can begin the structural appraisal. This may involve more than one stage. A preliminary investigation is useful to note any obvious signs of distress and perhaps to plan the more detailed survey. But just as there is no point in killing the patient in order to determine the cause of the disease, a surveyor is not an archaeologist, and complete dismantling of the building in order to describe it is not possible. Thus, complete knowledge of the building's particular anatomy will not be possible and the investigation, necessarily limited, needs to be directed towards the eventual aims. Thus some judgement has to be exercised in determining the extent of the opening up that may be necessary. More specifically, it may not be possible to determine either the structural properties of the materials or the nature of the connections within the structure.

In a structural appraisal one is first looking for the load paths through the structure and then at the behaviour of individual components and connections. It has already been noted that there may be no clear load path, with the structure apparently standing by 'force of habit'. Where this is so the conservator may be concerned to establish an appropriate load path though the structure and so be concerned with the condition of structural members that will in consequence be loaded. It will be clear from what has been said in Chapter 4 that the load path through the structure can change with time. In a timber structure an indication of which members are loaded can sometimes be obtained by looking at movement at the joints and sometimes by examining their deflections.

The determination of the condition of individual timbers can present a problem. If the timbers have been dismantled they can be examined with ease in the workshop, whereas it may be difficult to inspect all sides of a timber on site. Opening up the structure for inspection might be at the expense of the loss of secondary material that also has historic significance: the removal of part of a wattle and daub wall, a lime-ash floor or a decorative plaster ceiling, for example. There are a number of more obvious places to examine that are both vulnerable to decay and are structurally critical. The heel joints of softwood trusses are one example. The use of a decay-detecting drill is the common solution to this, but the survey needs to provide sufficient information for the design of the repairs and not simply locate areas of decay. If the survey is to provide sufficiently detailed information for the carpenter and/or engineer it should be carried out with some knowledge of the load transmission mechanism within the structure to ensure that critical members are examined. Moreover, it is important to be responsive to what is found. When decay is found it is sensible to carry out a more detailed survey in that area, with a close pattern of drilling to determine its extent.

Reporting

Again, rather like the doctor, the object is not to produce a perfect spec-imen at the end but simply to ensure that the subject is in reasonably good health. What this means for a building is that one is aiming to give the structure a helping hand and not to bring it up to the standards of modern codes of practice. If the structure has survived and there is no sign of continuing decay or the continuation of some action that is causing distress, then the chances are that it will continue to survive. Leave well alone. Assessing a building against modern codes and then making it conform to them may do irreparable harm to the historic fabric. The remedies proposed should also be appropriate to the nature of the problem. Amputation at the knee is not an appropriate treatment for an ingrown toenail, although remedies proposed for building prob-lems sometimes have something of this character.

ISCARSAH takes the view that there needs to be an **explanatory report** explaining why the actions recommended are required. This needs to be conveyed to the client in such a way that he or she can make decisions on a course of action, just as the doctor needs to explain pro-posed or alternative treatments to a patient. This can mean presenting the report in simple terms and explaining the structural problems in a way that they can be understood. Such explanations may have to be made to other professional advisors (such as the architect), to conserva-tion officers (if it is a building of historic significance), and to the client. The building belongs to the client and ultimately it is the client who should be placed in a position in which he or she can make sensible decisions about the advice given.

Bibliography

ALCOCK, N. W. (1981). *Cruck Construction*. Council for British Archaeology Research Report 42.

ALEXANDER, S. J. (2002). Imposed floor loading for offices: a re-appraisal. *The Structural Engineer*, 3 December, 35–45.

AMERICAN INSTITUTE OF TIMBER CONSTRUCTION (1985). *Timber Construction Manual*, 3rd edn. New York: Wiley.

BAIRD, J. A. and OZELTON, E. C. (1984). *Timber Designers' Manual*, 2nd edn. London: Granada.

BARLOW, P. (1817). *An essay on the strength and stress of timber, founded upon experiments performed at the Royal Military Academy*. London: J. Taylor.

BARNWELL, P. T. and ADAMS, A. T. (1994). *The House Within*. London: HMSO.

BLASS, H. J., AUNE, P., CHOO, B. S., GORLACHER, R., GRIFFITH, D. R., HILSON, B., RACHER, P. and STECK, G. (eds.) (1995). *Timber Engineering: STEP 1*. The Netherlands: Centrum Hout.

BOOTH, L. G. and REECE, P. O. (1967). *The Structural Use of Timber, A Commentary on the British Standard Code of Practice CP112*. London: Spon.

BRUNGRABER, R. L. (1985). Traditional timber joinery: a modern analysis. *PhD Thesis*, Stanford University.

BRUNSKILL, R. (1985). *Timber-frame Building in Britain*. London: Gollancz.

CHARLES, F. W. B. (1967). *Medieval Cruck-Building and its Derivatives*. London: Society for Medieval Archaeology.

CHARLES, F. W. B. (1970). The medieval timber-frame tradition. In Berger, R. (ed.) *Scientific Methods in Medieval Archaeology*, pp. 213–237. Los Angeles: University of California.

CHARLES, F. W. B. (1974a). Scotches, lever sockets and rafter holes. *Vernacular Architecture*, **5**, 21–24.

CHARLES, F. W. B. (1974b). The timber framed buildings of Coventry: 169 Spon Street. *Birmingham and Warwickshire Archaeological Society Transactions*, **86**, 113–131.

CHARLES, F. W. B. and CHARLES, M. (1995). *Conservation of timber buildings*. Shaftesbury: Donhead.

COONEY, E. W. (1991). Eighteenth century Britain's missing sawmills: a blessing in disguise? *Construction History*, **7**, 29–46.

CORDINGLEY, R. A. (1961). British historical roof types and their members. *Transactions of the Ancient Monuments Society*, **9**, 73–117.

DAWES, M. and YEOMANS, D. (1985). Timber trussed girders. *The Structural Engineer*, **63a**(5), 147–154.

DE L'ORME, P. (1561). *Novelles Inventions de Bien Bastir*. Paris.

ENGLISH HERITAGE (1996). *Office Floor Loading in Historic Buildings*. Swindon.

FOOT, N. D. J., LITTON, C. D. and SIMPSON, W. G. (1986). The high roofs of the east end of Lincoln Cathedral. *Medieval Art and Architecture at Lincoln Cathedral* (B.A.A. Conf. Trans. 8), 47–74.

FOREST PRODUCTS LABORATORY (1974). *Wood Handbook: Wood as an Engineering Material*. Agricultural Handbook 72, US Government Printing Office, Washington DC.

GUNTHER, R. T. (1928). *The Architecture of Sir Roger Pratt*. Oxford.

HARRIS, R. (1989). The grammar of carpentry. *Vernacular Architecture*, **20**, 1–8.

HEWETT, C. (1980). *English Historic Carpentry*. London and Chichester: Phillimore.

HEYMAN, J. (1976). An apsidal timber roof at Westminster. *Gesta*, **15**, 53–60. Reprinted in *Arches, Vaults and Buttresses*, Variorum, 1996.

HORN, W. and CHARLES, F. W. B. (1966). The cruck-built barn of Middle Littleton in Worcestershire, England. *Journal of the Society of Architectural Historians*, **25**, 21–39.

HORN, W. and CHARLES, F. W. B. (1973). The cruck-built barn of Leigh Court, Worcestershire, England. *Journal of the Society of Architectural Historians*, **32**, 5–29.

JONES, R. (1997). Upgrading of timber members in historic buildings. *Journal of the Institute of Wood Science*, **14**(4), 192–203.

JONES, R. and SMEDLEY, D. (2000). Replacement of decayed beam ends with epoxy-bonded timber composites: structural testing. *The Structural Engineer*, **78**(15), 19–22.

LAVERS, G. M. (1969). *The Strength Properties of Timbers*, 2nd edn. Forest Products Research Bulletin No. 50. London: HMSO.

MCDOWALL, R. W., SMITH, J. T. and STELL, C. F. (1966). Westminster Abbey: the timber roofs of the Collegiate Church of St Peter at Westminster. *Archaeologia*, **100**, 155–174.

MERCER, E. (1975). *English Vernacular Houses*. London: HMSO.

METTEM, C. J. and MILNER, M. (2000). *Resin Repairs to Timber Structures; Vol 1, Guidance and Selection*. TRADA Technology Report 3/2000.

MITCHELL, G. R. and WOODGATE, R. W. (1971). Floor loadings in office buildings – the results of a survey. *BRE Current Paper 3/71*, Building Research Establishment.

NELSON, L. H. (1996). Early wooden truss connections vs. Wood shrinkage: from mortise-and-tenon joints to bolted connections. *Association for Preservation Technology Bulletin*, **27**, 11–23.

NICHOLSON, P. (1792). *New Carpenter's Guide*. London.

NEWLANDS, J. (c1850) .*The Carpenter's Assistant*. Glasgow.

OZELTON, E. C. and BAIRD, J. A. (1976). *Timber Designers' Manual*. London: Granada.

PRICE, F. (1733). *The British Carpenter: or, a Treatise on Carpentry*.

RIDOUT, B. (1999). *Timber Decay in Buildings*. London: Spon.

SMITH, J. T. (1957). Medieval roofs: a classification. *Archaeological Journal*, **115**, 111–149.

TREDGOLD, T. (1820). *Elementary Principles of Carpentry*. London: John Weale.

WOOD, M. (1965), *The English Medieval House*. London. Reprinted 1981, London: Ferndale.

YEOMANS, D. (1989). Structural carpentry in London building. In Hobhouse, H. and Saunders, A. (eds.) *Good and Proper Materials: The Fabric of London since the Great Fire*, pp. 38–47. London: RCHM and London Topographical Society.

YEOMANS, D. (1991) British and American approaches to a roofing problem. *Journal of the Society of Architectural Historians*, **50**, 266–272.

YEOMANS, D. (1992a). *The Trussed Roof: its History and Development*. Aldershot: Scolar.

YEOMANS, D. (1992b). *The Architect and the Carpenter*. London: RIBA.

YEOMANS, D. (1999). The problems of assessing historic timber strengths using modern design codes. In Sickels-Taves, L. (ed.) *The Use of and Need for Preservation Standards in Architectural Conservation*, ASTM STP 1355, 119–127.

YEOMANS, D. and SMITH, A. (2000). Alternative strategies in restoring a medieval barn. In Kelley, S. (ed.) *Wood Structures: An East-West Forum on the Treatment, Conservation and Repair of Cultural Heritage*, ASTM STP 1351, 176–187.

British Standards

BS 373: 1929, Methods of testing small clear specimens of timber.

BS 4978: 1973, Timber grades for structural use.

BS 5268: Part 2: 1984, Structural use of timber. Code of practice, Permissible stress design, materials and workmanship. Subsequent editions referred to here are those appearing in 1996 and 2002.

BS 5268: Part 4: Section 4.1: 1978. Method of calculating fire resistance of timber members.

BS 5756: 1997, Visual strength grading of hardwood.

CP112: Part 2: 1971, The Structural use of timber: Metric units.

Appendix 1

Timber grades

The strength of a piece of timber depends upon the species and the grade. Thus a poor grade of a very good timber may have better strength properties than a good grade of a very poor timber. Because modern timber engineers may be indifferent to the species actually supplied and be interested only in the strength characteristics, modern design codes allow timbers to be specified according to strength classes. The commonly used strength classes for softwoods will be in the range C16–C24 (Table A1). The lower of these includes the GS grades of redwood and whitewood and imported Douglas fir, while the higher one covers the SS grades of these timbers. The GS grade of western red cedar only reaches the C14 strength class, while its SS grade is C18 strength class. At the same time this strength class includes the GS grade of Caribbean pitch pine, whose SS grade is strength class C27.

These grades have been developed for modern supplies. For example, hem-fir and spruce-pine-fir are mixed species obtained from

Species	Strength class					
	C14	C16	C18	C22	C24	C27
Caribbean pitch pine			GS			SS
Redwood/whitewood		GS			SS	
Douglas fir-larch		GS			SS	
Western red cedar	GS		SS			
Hem-fir		GS			SS	
Spruce-pine-fir		GS			SS	
British pine	GS			SS		
British spruce	GS		SS			

Table A1 Extracted from BS 5268, Table 2.

Canada and the USA. These sources are quite different from historical sources and the species correspondingly different from those found in historic buildings.

Appendix 2

Diagrams for visual grading and grade limits

With the knots and other features measured (Figure A1) these can be used to grade the timber.

Growth rate

The limit on the number of growth rings/inch that is applied to softwoods, where faster growth results in lower strength, will probably not be significant for historic timbers. Experience suggests that these generally fall within the limits for 75 grade.

Softwood grade	Number of growth rings/25 mm
75	8
65	6
50	4
40	4

Note that, unlike softwoods, fast grown hardwoods are denser and stronger than slowly grown hardwoods.

Fissures

The sizes of fissures are not limited by BS 5756, but for both hardwood and softwood CP112 limits them as follows:

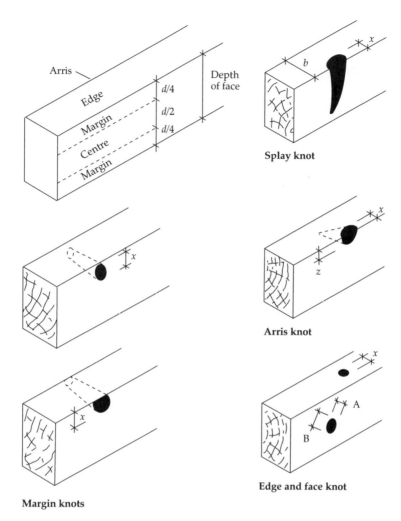

Splay knot

Arris knot

Edge and face knot

Margin knots

Figure A1 Definition of different types of knots. In each case x, or both x and z in the case of arris knots, indicates the dimension to be measured. For an arris knot the size used is x + z/3. For a knot running from the edge to the face the face dimension to be used should be the average of A and B, which are the maximum and minimum dimensions of the knot.

Grade	Maximum size as a fraction of the thickness of the member
75	0.3
65	0.4
50	0.5
40	0.6

Slope of grain

Slope of grain is limited as follows:

Grade	Maximum slope of grain
75	1 in 14
65	1 in 11
50	1 in 8
40	1 in 6

Wane

Wane can be a problem for existing oak frame buildings, but is not usually a problem in repair timbers, which can be selected to exclude it. Neither is it normally a problem in large section historic softwood structures, where there is generally little if any wane.

Grade	Maximum wane as a fraction of the surface
75	0.1
65	0.1
50	0.2
40	0.2

Knots

Table A2 shows knot limits for timbers graded to CP112.

Allowable stresses for groups of softwoods

CP112 provided a table of allowable stresses for individual species of timbers (Table A3), but for convenience also grouped softwoods into three species groups. Of these the conservator is more likely to be dealing with the first two and also with dry rather than green timber. Species group S1 is Douglas fir, Pitch pine and Larch. Group S2 is Western hemlock, Parana pine, Scots pine, Norway spruce and Canadian spruce.

Width of surface	Edge arris and splay				Margin knots				Face knots				Compression members			
	75	65	50	40	75	65	50	40	75	65	50	40	75	65	50	40
16	4	6	8	11				6	4	7	9	10	4	7	9	10
19	5	7	9	13			4	7	5	8	10	11	5	8	10	11
22	6	8	11	14			5	8	6	9	11	13	6	9	11	13
25	7	9	13	16			6	9	6	10	13	15	6	10	13	15
32	8	12	16	20		4	8	11	8	12	16	18	8	12	16	18
36	9	13	18	22		5	9	12	9	13	17	20	9	13	17	20
38	10	14	19	23		6	10	13	10	14	18	21	10	14	18	21
40	10	15	20	24		6	10	14	10	15	19	22	10	15	19	22
44	11	16	22	26	4	8	12	15	11	16	21	24	11	16	21	24
50	13	18	25	29	5	9	14	17	13	19	23	27	13	19	23	27
63	16	23	31	37	7	12	18	21	16	23	29	33	16	23	29	33
75	19	28	37	43	9	16	21	25	19	27	34	39	19	27	34	39
100	25	37	50	56	13	20	29	33	25	35	45	51	25	35	45	51
125	31	47	63	69	17	25	37	41	32	43	56	64	32	43	56	64
150	37	56	75	83	20	30	44	48	38	51	66	74	38	51	66	74
175	41	61	82	88	24	34	52	56	44	59	75	84	44	59	75	84
200	44	66	87	93	28	39	59	64	50	66	85	94	50	66	85	94
225	47	70	92	97	32	44	67	72	55	72	92	101	55	72	92	101
250	51	75	97	102	35	48	75	79	60	78	99	108	60	78	99	108
300	54	79	107	112	40	59	88	92	69	91	114	122	69	91	114	122

Table A2 Knot limits for timbers graded to CP112 (from CP112, Table 62).

Species group	S1					S2				
	Basic	75	65	50	40	Basic	75	65	50	40
Bending and tension parallel to the grain	17.2	12.1	10.3	7.9	6.2	13.8	9.7	7.9	6.2	5.2
Compression parallel to the grain	13.1	9.3	7.6	5.5	4.5	11	7.9	6.6	4.8	3.8
Compression perpendicular to the grain	2.48	2.21	2.21	1.93	1.93	2.07	1.72	1.72	1.52	1.52
Shear parallel to the grain	1.52	1.14	0.97	0.76	0.62	1.52	1.14	0.97	0.76	0.62
E Mean	9700					8300				
E Minimum	4800					4500				

Figures are all in N/mm^2.

Table A3 Allowable stresses for dry timbers (from CP 112, Table 11).

Appendix 3

Comparative loads on a pegged tenon

Refer to Figure 3.1.

Consider a peg of diameter ϕ driven though a tenon of thickness t.

Then if the allowable crushing strength is f_1 the maximum load on the peg $= f_1 t \phi$.

Consider now the shear towards the end of the tenon.

Let the length to the end $= l$.

If the timber is sheared towards the end of the tenon there are two planes of failure, and if the allowable stress in shear along the grain $= f_2$, the load that can be carried $= 2 l t f_2$.

Theoretically, failure in both crushing and shear will occur if:

$$f_1 t \phi = 2 l t f_2$$

The values for f_1 and f_2 for oak are 4 and 2 N/mm^2 respectively, so that substituting these in the formula above gives

$$4 t \phi = 4 l t$$

In other words the length to the end of the timber has to be equal to or greater than the diameter of the peg, assuming that we want crushing of the peg to occur before shear failure of the timber in the tenon.

The other mode of failure is shear in the peg, and here there are again two planes of failure, the area of each being $= \pi \phi^2 / 4$.

To find the allowable load the average shear stress has to be multiplied by a form factor to take account of the varying shear stress across the peg. For a circular peg the form factor is 0.75 (the maximum shear stress being $4/3 \times$ the average shear stress). Thus the allowable load $= 2 f_2 \pi \phi^2 / 4 \times 3/4 = 3/8 f_2 \pi \phi^2$.

Again, substituting the values from BS 5268 and comparing this with crushing in the peg:

$$4 t \phi = 3/8 \times 2 \pi \phi^2 \quad \text{from which} \quad t = 3/16 \pi \phi \approx 0.6 \phi$$

In fact, the thickness of the tenon is normally much larger than this suggesting that the limit on the load on a mortice and tenon in tension would be governed by the shear strength of the peg.

Appendix 4

Hankinson's formula

Allowable stresses in compression and the allowable loads on fasteners are given for the load applied perpendicular to the grain and parallel to the grain. The allowable stress in compression is much lower when the load is applied perpendicular to the grain. Fastener loads are much more affected by the direction of loading in softwoods than for hardwood. Hankinson's formula is applied to find both allowable compression stresses and fastener loads when the direction of loading is at an angle to the grain. The formula is:

$$N_\theta = PQ/(P\sin^2\theta + Q\cos^2\theta)$$

where N_θ = value of the allowable stress or load at angle θ to the grain, P = value of the stress or load parallel to the grain, and Q = value of the stress or load perpendicular to the grain.

Index